T0214164

Lecture Notes in Computer Science   11847

More information about this series at http://www.springer.com/series/7407

Pierre Ganty · Mohamed Kaâniche (Eds.)

Verification and Evaluation of Computer and Communication Systems

13th International Conference, VECoS 2019
Porto, Portugal, October 9, 2019
Proceedings

 Springer

Editors
Pierre Ganty 🆔
IMDEA Software Institute
Pozuelo de Alarcón, Spain

Mohamed Kaâniche 🆔
Laboratory for Analysis and Architecture
Toulouse, France

ISSN 0302-9743   ISSN 1611-3349   (electronic)
Lecture Notes in Computer Science
ISBN 978-3-030-35091-8   ISBN 978-3-030-35092-5   (eBook)
https://doi.org/10.1007/978-3-030-35092-5

LNCS Sublibrary: SL1 – Theoretical Computer Science and General Issues

This Springer imprint is published by the registered company Springer Nature Switzerland AG
The registered company address is: Gewerbestrasse 11, 6330 Cham, Switzerland

Preface

These proceedings include the papers presented at the 13th International Conference on Verification and Evaluation of Computer and Communication Systems (VECoS 2019), held at Porto, Portugal, on October 9, 2019. This year VECoS is colocated with the International Symposium on Formal Methods, FM 2019.

The first edition of the conference, VECoS 2007, took place in Algiers, VECoS 2008 in Leeds, VECoS 2009 in Rabat, VECoS 2010 in Paris, VECoS 2011 in Tunis, VECoS 2012 in Paris, VECoS 2013 in Florence, VECoS 2014 in Bejaia, VECoS 2015 in Bucharest, VECoS 2016 in Tunis, VECoS 2017 in Montreal, and VECoS 2018 in Grenoble.

The aim of the VECoS conference is to bring together researchers and practitioners in the areas of verification, control, performance, and dependability evaluation in order to discuss the state of the art and challenges in modern computer and communication systems in which functional and extra-functional properties are strongly interrelated. Thus, the main motivation for VECoS is to encourage the cross-fertilization between various formal verification and evaluation approaches, methods, and techniques, and especially those developed for concurrent and distributed hardware/software systems.

The Program Committee (PC) of VECoS 2019 included researchers from 20 countries. We received 13 full submissions from 10 countries. After a thorough and lively discussion phase, the PC decided to accept seven papers. The conference program also included two invited talks. The invited speakers were: Jose F. Morales from the IMDEA Software Institute, Spain; and Ali Mili from the New Jersey Institute of Technology, NY, USA.

We are grateful to the Program and Organizing Committee members, to the reviewers for their cooperation, and to Springer for their professional support during the production phase of the proceedings. We are also thankful to all authors of submitted papers and to all participants of the conference. Their interest in this conference and contributions are greatly appreciated.

August 2019

Pierre Ganty
Mohamed Kaâniche

Organization

VECoS 2019 is organized in Porto and colocated with the International Symposium on Formal Methods, FM 2019.

Organizing Committee

Program Co-chairs

Pierre Ganty	IMDEA Software Institute, Spain
Mohamed Kaâniche	LAAS-CNRS, France

Local Organization Chair

José Nuno Oliveira	University of Minho, Portugal

Publicity Co-chairs

Belgacem Ben Hedia	CEA-LIST Saclay, France
Vladimir-Alexandru Paun	ENSTA ParisTech, France

Steering Committee

Djamil Aissani	LAMOS, Université de Bejaia, Algeria
Mohamed Faouzi Atig	Uppsala University, Sweden
Kamel Barkaoui (Chair)	CEDRIC CNAM Paris, France
Hanifa Boucheneb	Veriform, Polytechnique Montreal, Canada
Francesco Flammini	Ansaldo STS, Milano, Italy
Belgacem Ben Hedia	LIST CEA Saclay, Paris, France
Mohamed Kaâniche	LAAS-CNRS, France
Bruno Monsuez	ENSTA UIIS, France
Nihal Pekergin	LACL, Université Paris-Est Créteil, France
Tayssir Touili	LIPN, CNRS, Université Paris-Nord, France

Program Committee

A. Aljarbouh	S. Bliudze	B. van Gastel
D. Aissani	P. Bonhomme	G. Geeraerts
Y. Ait Ameur	H. Boucheneb	S. Genaim
M. F. Atig	Yu-F. Chen	A. Geniet
E. Badouel	F. Chu	M. Ghazel
K. Barkaoui	G. Ciobanu	S. Haddad
A. Benzina	A. Fantechi	I. Ben Hafaiedh
S. Bernardi	P. Ganty (Chair)	B. Ben Hedia

R. Iosif	M. Lauer	A. Rezine
M. Jmaiel	R. Meyer	A. Sangnier
J. Julvez	A. Mili	S. M. de Sousa
P. Katsaros	A. Nouri	M. Stoelinga
M. Kaâniche (Chair)	C. Pagetti	T. Touili
M. Krichen	V. A. Paun	K. Wolf
L. Kristensen	J. S. Pinto	K. Wolter

Additional Reviewers

Hsin-Hung Lin
Stefanos Skalistis
Waheed Ahmad

Keynote Abstracts

Top-Down Horn Clause-Based Program Analysis in the Ciao Language

Jose F. Morales

IMDEA Software Institute
josef.morales@imdea.org

Abstract. Ciao is a logic programming language which was designed from the root to be extensible, support multiparadigm features, and provide the flexibility of a dynamic language, but with guaranteed safety, reliability, and efficiency. A key component of Ciao is its preprocessor (CiaoPP), a context-sensitive, abstract interpretation-based analyzer based on inferring via fixpoint computation the abstract program semantics, over a set of user-definable abstract domains. In this talk I will introduce the Ciao/CiaoPP approach, and recent results on the use of assertions to guide such fixpoint computations, incremental and modular analysis, optimization of run-time checks and static analysis of their cost, combination with automated testing, as well as other applications like semantic code search, multilanguage analysis based on transforming both high- and low-level program representations into Horn clauses, or energy consumption verification.

1968 to 2019: Half a Century of Correctness Enhancement

Ali Mili

New Jersey Institute of Technology (NJIT)
ali.mili@njit.edua

Abstract. Whereas correctness preservation is considered as the gold standard of software engineering processes, in this talk we argue that in fact the vast majority of software engineering processes do not involve correctness preservation but rather correctness enhancement. We explore some mathematics of correctness enhancement, discuss in what way and to what extent correctness enhancement pervades software engineering, and tentatively speculate about prospects for using these insights to enhance software engineering practice.

Contents

Modeling Concurrent Behaviors as Words

Yohan Boichut, Jean-Michel Couvreur$^{(\boxtimes)}$, Xavier Ferry,
and Mohamadou Tafsir Sakho

Laboratoire d'Informatique Fondamentale d'Orléans, Université d'Orléans,
45067 Orleans Cedex 2, France
{yohan.boichut,jean-michel.couvreur,xavier.ferry,
mohamadoutafsir.sakho}@univ-orleans.fr

Abstract. Performing formal verification of concurrent systems involves partial order logics (here MSO with partial orders) for the specification of properties or of the concurrent system itself. A common structure for the verification of concurrent systems is so-called pomset. A pomset is a multiset of partially ordered events. The partial order relation describes causal dependencies of events. We propose a new word based model, namely Pre-Post-Pomset, making the exploration of pomsets space possible. In this paper, our new model stands to be a general model in the sense that some classical models used in the specification of concurrent systems (Synchronized product of systems, Mazurkiewicz traces or parallel series) can be specified within. Besides its general aspect, our model offers decidability results on the verification problem according to an MSO formula on pomsets.

Keywords: Partial order · Pomset · Specification · Models · Concurrent systems

1 Introduction

Since forty years, verification has been a very fruitful research area whose results have been applied on a multitude of critical systems, e.g. aircraft embedded systems, automated transport subways, security protocols, etc. The research topics relate to the conception of new specification languages on one hand and the verification techniques on the other hand. For the former, in order to describe formally a system, its behavior or the expected properties, some specification languages (PROMELA [9], TLA [10], ...) have been introduced.

Nowaday, some matured tools are available: SPIN [9] or SMV [14] for instance. Such tools have been developed and have integrated new techniques. These improvements, such as abstraction, symbolic verification, bounded model-checking or partial order reduction, have made these tools more and more efficient and able to handle more and more sophisticated systems. All the work around these verification techniques is probably a consequence of the mastery of the theoretical tools linking logic, automata [22] and μ-calculus [4] on simple

© Springer Nature Switzerland AG 2019
P. Ganty and M. Kaâniche (Eds.): VECoS 2019, LNCS 11847, pp. 1–15, 2019.
https://doi.org/10.1007/978-3-030-35092-5_1

structures such as words and trees. The application of these techniques is done on a simple model adopted by the whole community: the transition systems. Beyond the community itself, these techniques are understandable by engineers, researchers and students at such a point that developing a verification prototype is now a master's degree exercise.

Despite many works around the analysis of concurrent systems and their logics integrating the event causality, an efficient reference tool does not exist. Indeed, each of these works is based on specific models, such as Petri nets [6,18,19,21], Mazurkiewicz traces [8,12,16], product of systems [2,20], parallel series [11] or Message Sequence Charts graphs [15,17]. Apparently, there is no model arising from the multitude. However, all of these models rely on concurrency semantics founded on a theoretical model, i.e. pomsets. Moreover, monadic second order (MSO) logics are used for the specification of properties. In order to get decidability results on these models, two techniques seem to emerge: (1) extending decidability results obtained on words [23] and (2) applying graph rewriting general results [7] to transform decidability issues into problems on trees. Surprisingly, one may note that these techniques are well mastered by classic model-checking tools with optimization techniques but such an effort is still missing in the context of analysis of concurrent systems. From our point of view, the major obstacle to develop such techniques lies in the lack of a model for concurrent systems as simple as the transition systems are for other systems.

Starting from the assessment that pomsets constitute a theoretical tool omnipresent behind all existing models, we propose in this paper a new model, the so-called Pre-Post-Pomsets. A Pre-Post-Pomset is a word or a regular expression (specifying a regular set of words) whose interpretation is a pomset or a regular set of pomsets. Moreover, our model is expressive enough for specifying classical models such as Mazurkiewicz traces, parallel series, Message Sequence Charts or synchronized system product. Thus, a system is reduced to a simple regular expression. A direct consequence is that the verification of an MSO formula on this model is decidable. Notice that in our study, we consider models as a set of pomsets instead of a branching structure like event structure [19].

The paper is organized as follows: in Sect. 2, we recall some basic definitions on words, pomsets and MSO formulas. In Sect. 3, our new model and its elementary model, i.e. Pre-Post-Pomsets, are introduced. Moreover, we develop a composition operation on Pre-Post-Pomsets in Sect. 4. It is a critical issue in the sense that the specification of complicated systems may be made easier thanks to such operation. And finally, in Sect. 5, we specify some of the classical models with Pre-Post-Pomsets.

2   Basic Definitions

In this section, we quickly recall the definition of monadic second-order logic and mention some of its basic properties. We assume that the reader is familiar with the basic notions of logic.

Monadic second-order logic (MSO) is the extension of *first-order logic* (FO) by set variables $X, Y, \ldots$ ranging over sets of positions, quantifiers $\exists X$, $\forall X$ over such variables, and membership tests $Y(x)$ (i.e. $x \in Y$).

A (finite or infinite) word over an alphabet Σ is considered as a structure whose universe is the set of positions $[\sigma]$ where $[\sigma] = \{i \in \mathbb{N} : 0 \le i < |\sigma|\}$. Moreover, this structure provided with the order relation $\le$ and the predicates $a^?$ with $a \in \Sigma$ such that $a^?(i)$ means that the letter occurring at position i is a. We also denote by $\sigma(i)$ the letter occurring in σ at position i. The empty word is represented by $\emptyset$. And for two words σ and σ', we denote by $\sigma \cdot \sigma'$ their concatenation. The relationship between regular languages of (finite or infinite) words and MSO-definable languages is given by Büchi theorems [5].

Theorem 1. *A language of (finite or infinite) words is regular if and ony if it is expressible in MSO logic.*

Roughly speaking, given an MSO formula $\phi(X_1, \ldots, X_n)$ of arity n where the variables X_i with $i = 1, \ldots, n$ represent sets of integers, there exists a regular language over the alphabet $\{0, 1\}^n$ representing the set of instantiations of variables $X_1, \ldots, X_n$ satisfying the formula $\phi(X_1, \ldots, X_n)$. Reciprocally, such a regular language can be specified by an MSO formula. A corollary of this result is the decidability of the satisfaction of MSO formulas over words and the verification problem of regular languages with respect to an MSO formula.

Let E be a universe and P be the set of unary predicates defined over E. The set P is considered as a set of predicates stating that a given property is fulfilled by a given vertex i.e. for a predicate $p^? \in P$ and a vertex s, if $p^?(s)$ then the vertex s has the property p. A graph is $S = (E, P, \rightarrow)$ where E and P are defined as above and $\rightarrow$ a binary relation.

Given such a graph $S = (E, P, \rightarrow)$ and $B \subseteq E$, we denote by $S_{|B} = (B, P_{|B}, \rightarrow_{|B})$ the subgraph such that $P_{|B} \subseteq P$ and $\rightarrow_{|B}$ iff $x \rightarrow_{|B} y \equiv x \in B \wedge y \in B \wedge x \rightarrow y$. The substructure $S_{|B}$ is called a restriction of S on B. Given an unary MSO formula φ, we denote $S_{|\varphi}$ the restriction of S on the set of vertex which fulfill φ. The following proposition claims that restrictions can be useful for the verification of formulas on graph languages.

Proposition 1. *Let L be a language of graphs for a given set of elementary predicats P and let φ be an unary MSO formula on graphs in L. Let $L_{|\varphi} = \{G_{|\varphi} | G \in L\}$ be the language of graph restrictions on φ. Let ϕ be an MSO formula on graphs in $L_{|\varphi}$. There exists a formula ϕ_φ such that $\forall G \in L : G_{|\varphi} \models \phi \Leftrightarrow G \models \phi_\varphi$.*

A pomset is a graph where the binary relation is a partial order. Usually, elements of the universe are called events and the relation is denoted $\preceq$. We assume that the events of a pomset have finite past (*i.e.* $\forall e \in E : |\{e' \in E : e' \preceq e\}| < \infty$).

When needed, a graph $S = (E, P, \rightarrow)$ where transitive closure $\xrightarrow{*}$ defines a partial order satisfying the finite past constraint may be considered as a pomset. Notice that the transitive closure $\xrightarrow{*}$ is definable in MSO. Another important binary relation is the immediate successor $\prec\cdot$ which is also definable in MSO. The negative result on pomsets is that the satisfaction problem of an MSO formula is undecidable in general [3].

Example 1. Figures 1 and 2 give the representations of two simple pomsets.

Notice that $a_0 \preceq a_2$ for the two pomsets. Moreover they have the same $\preceq$ relation restricted to non ϵ-events. However, the immediate successor $\prec\cdot$ are not equal for non ϵ-events.

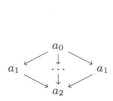

Fig. 1. Simple pomset.

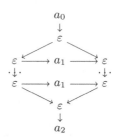

Fig. 2. Pomset with ϵ-events.

3   Pre-Post-Pomsets

In the previous section, we have mentioned that the satisfaction problem of MSO formulas on pomsets is undecidable in general. Nevertheless, on regular sets or finite sets of pomsets, it becomes decidable as well as the inherent verification problem. However, we need a new structure in order to represent pomsets and in a more general way, regular sets of pomsets. So, let us introduce the notion of Pre-Post-Pomsets.

Let Γ and Σ be respectively a finite set of marks and a finite alphabet. Basically, a Pre-Post-Pomset is a word where each letter is a tuple (pre, a, post) where $a \in \Sigma$ is the event label and pre and post are sets of marks used to encode the partial order relation. Through this partial order relation, we are able to associate a unique pomset to the Pre-Post-Pomsets.

Definition 1. *Let Γ and Σ be respectively a finite set of marks and a finite alphabet. Let Σ_Γ be the alphabet composed of tuples* (pre, a, post) *such that* pre $\subseteq$ Γ, post $\subseteq \Gamma$ *and* $a \in \Sigma$. *A Pre-Post-Pomset π is a (finite or infinite) word on the alphabet Σ_Γ^*. One says that π is a Pre-Post-Pomset marked by Γ over Σ.*

Example 2. A Pre-Post-Pomset π can be represented as follows:

$$\pi = (\emptyset, a_0, e_0)(e_0, a_1, e_1)(e_0, a_1, e_2) \cdots (e_0, a_1, e_n)(\{e_1, \cdots e_n\}, a_2, \emptyset)$$

with $\Sigma = \{a_0, a_1, a_2\}$ and $\Gamma = \{e_0, \cdots, e_n\}$.

Remark 1. For the sake of readability, we do not use braces on tuples $(pre, a, post)$ whenever *pre* or *post* is a singleton.

Definition 2 (toPomset). *Let* $\sigma \in \Sigma_\Gamma^*$ *be a (finite or infinite) Pre-Post-Pomset. Let* $\sigma_i = (\text{pre}_i, a_i, \text{post}_i)$ *be the letter at position i. We define* toPomset(σ) *as the pomset* $(E, P, \overset{*}{\rightarrow})$ *such that*

- *E is the set of positions of σ i.e. $E = [\sigma]$;*
- *P is the set of predicates $P = \{a^? \mid a \in \Sigma\}$ where $a^?(i) \Leftrightarrow a_i = a$ for any position $i \in [\sigma]$;*
- *For any $i, j \in [\sigma]$, $i \rightarrow j \Leftrightarrow \exists m \in \Gamma : i \overset{m}{\rightarrow} j$ where $i \overset{m}{\rightarrow} j = i < j \wedge$ $\text{post}_m(i) \wedge \text{pre}_m(j) \wedge (\forall k, i < k < j \Rightarrow \neg\text{post}_m(k))$, $\text{pre}_m(i) = (m \in \text{pre}_i)$ and $\text{post}_m(i) = (m \in \text{post}_i)$.*

Example 3. Let π be the Pre-Post-Pomset defined in Example 2. The pomset toPomset(π) is $(E, P, \preceq)$ with $E = [\pi] = \{0, \cdots, n + 1\}$, $P = \{a_0^?, a_1^?, a_2^?\}$ where $a_0^?(i) \Leftrightarrow i = 0$, $a_1^?(i) \Leftrightarrow 0 < i < n$, $a_2^?(i) \Leftrightarrow i = n + 1$ and $\preceq$ be the partial order defined such that $x \preceq y \Leftrightarrow (x, y) \in \{(0, 1), \cdots, (0, n), (0, n + 1), (1, n + 1), \cdots (n, n + 1)\}$. The pomset toPomset$(\pi)$ is the one represented in Fig. 1.

Theorem 2. *For any finite pomset $(E, P, \preceq)$, there exists a set of marks Γ, an alphabet Σ and a word $\sigma \in \Sigma_\Gamma^*$ such that* toPomset$(\sigma) = (E, P, \preceq)$.

Remark 2. In order to get a systematic translation from a Pre-Post-Pomset to a finite pomset, we use the set of events E as the set of marks Γ. This translation is far from being canonical, smarter translations can be obtained, depending on the nature of the pomset. Indeed in particular by reducing the size of Γ: in Example of Fig. 2, we could use only three marks.

We formalize the notion of regular languages of pomsets as regular languages of Pre-Post-Pomsets.

Definition 3. *Let Π be a set of (finite or infinite) pomsets. The set Π is regular if there exists a finite set of marks Γ, an alphabet Σ and a regular language L of Pre-Post-Pomsets such that* toPomset$(L) = \Pi$.

Since each event requires a limited number of immediate predecessors in Pre-Post-Pomsets, some structures do not seem specifiable with Pre-Post-Pomsets (see Fig. 1). As a workaround, one can use ε-events. In Fig. 2, note that each event has a bounded number of predecessors. This language of pomsets can be only specified through the use of ε-events. We hence introduce the notion of ϵ-regular languages of pomsets and give the expressiveness proposition.

Definition 4. *Let Π be a set of (finite or infinite) pomsets. The set Π is ϵ-regular language if there exists a finite set of marks Γ, an alphabet Σ and a regular language L of Pre-Post-Pomsets over the alphabet $\Sigma \cup \{\epsilon\}$ such that* toPomset$(L)_{|\neg\epsilon^?} = \Pi$.

Proposition 2. $\varepsilon-$*regular languages of Pre-Post-Pomsets are strictly more expressive than regular languages of Pre-Post-Pomsets.*

We conclude this part with the main theorem which is a direct consequence of Theorem 1 and Proposition 1.

Theorem 3. *The verification problem on regular and $\varepsilon-$regular languages of Pre-Post-Pomsets with respect to a MSO formula on pomsets is decidable.*

4 Composing Pre-Post-Pomsets

We now introduce the notion of composition of Pre-Post-Pomsets. Composition is a theoretical tool commonly used for the description of complex systems [1]. In particular, in our context, composition makes the specification of some classical models for concurrent systems (like MSC or parallel series) easier. Considering a Pre-Post-Pomset as a word, the basic idea of our composition is to substitute a letter of this word by a Pre-Post-Pomset. Interpreting these words as pomsets, it remains to carefully substitute an event (a vertex in the graph representation) by a pomset. Here, *carefully substitute* means that the dependency relation of the original pomset has to be preserved after the homomorphism application.

Hence, the Pre-Post-Pomset on which we apply the substitution has to fulfill some criteria explained in Definition 7. We first need to introduce some definitions in order to check whether a substitution is well formed.

Given a Pre-Post-Pomset π and a mark m of π, let us define the sets input_m and output_m. Informally, these two sets represent sets of events that may induce unexpected causality relations after having plugged π into another Pre-Post-Pomset by composition.

Definition 5. *Let π be a Pre-Post-Pomset over Σ marked by Γ. The input and output events for a mark m are defined by:*

$$\text{input}_\pi(m) = \{i \in [\pi] : \text{pre}_m(i) \wedge \forall j, j < i \Rightarrow \neg\text{post}_m(j)\}$$
$$\text{output}_\pi(m) = \{i \in [\pi] : \text{post}_m(i) \wedge \forall j, j > i \Rightarrow \neg\text{pre}_m(j)\}$$

Example 4. Considering $\Sigma = \{e_0, e_1, e_2\}$ and $\Gamma = \{a, b, c, 1, 2\}$, let π be the Pre-Post-Pomset $(\{a, b\}, e_0, \{1, 2\})(1, e_1, \emptyset)(2, e_2, \{c\})$ whose pomset $\text{toPomset}(\pi)$ is represented Fig. 3. Consequently, $\text{input}_\pi(a) = \{0\}$, $\text{input}_\pi(b) = \{0\}$ and $\text{input}_\pi(c) = \emptyset$. Moreover, $\text{input}_\pi(1) = \text{input}_\pi(2) = \emptyset$. Similarly, one can note that $\text{output}_\pi(c) = \{2\}$, $\text{output}_\pi(1) = \text{output}_\pi(2) = \{0\}$ and $\text{output}_\pi(a) = \text{output}_\pi(b) = \emptyset$.

Example 5. Let π' be the Pre-Post-Pomset $(\emptyset, e'_0, a)(\emptyset, e'_1, b)(\{a, b\}, e'_2, c)$ $(c, e'_3, \emptyset)$ whose pomset $\text{toPomset}(\pi')$ is given Fig. 4. Focusing on the tuple $(\{a, b\}, e'_2, c)$ occurring in π' and corresponding to the circular area in Fig. 4, one can note that two marks a and b are required by e'_2 and the mark c occurs at a post position within. Potentially, the sub-Pre-Post-Pomset $(\{a, b\}, e'_2, c)$

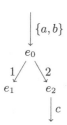

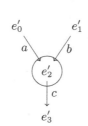

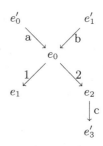

Fig. 3. toPomset(π) with input and output.

Fig. 4. toPomset(π') with input and output.

Fig. 5. toPomset($\Psi(\pi')$) with input and output.

could be substituted by the Pre-Post-Pomset π defined in Example 4. Indeed, input$_\pi(a) \neq \emptyset$, input$_\pi(b) \neq \emptyset$ and output$_\pi(c) \neq \emptyset$. So, one can note that π *behaves* as the sub-Pre-Post-Pomset $(\{a, b\}, e_2', c)$. Definition 6 simply adapts the notion of substitutions in the context of Pre-Post-Pomsets.

Definition 6. *Let Γ_1, Γ_2, Σ_1 and Σ_2 be respectively two sets of marks and two sets of events. A substitution Ψ is a homomorphism mapping any tuple (pre, a, post) in $2^{\Gamma_1} \times \Sigma_1 \times 2^{\Gamma_1}$ to a regular language of finite Pre-Post-Pomsets over Σ_2 marked by Γ_2. The substitution Ψ is naturally extended to any (finite or infinite) Pre-Post-Pomset and any regular languages of Pre-Post-Pomsets over Σ_1 marked by Γ_1.*

Definition 7 formally introduces the notion of safe substitution. The conditions under which such a homomorphism can be applied without adding unexpected causality relations or deleting expected causality relations.

Definition 7. *Let Ψ be a substitution from Pre-Post-Pomset over Σ_1 marked by Γ_1 to Pre-Post-Pomset over Σ_2 marked by Γ_2. Let π be a Pre-Post-Pomset over Σ_1 marked by Γ_1 such that $\pi = (\text{pre}_0, a_0, \text{post}_0) \cdots (\text{pre}_i, a_i, \text{post}_i) \cdots$. A substitution Ψ is safe with respect to π if the three following conditions hold:*

1. $\forall i \in [\pi], \forall m \notin \text{pre}_i : \text{input}_{\Psi(\text{pre}_i, a_i, \text{post}_i)}(m) = \emptyset$
2. $\forall i \in [\pi], \forall m \in \text{post}_i : \text{output}_{\Psi(\text{pre}_i, a_i, \text{post}_i)}(m) \neq \emptyset$
3. $\forall i, j \in [\pi], \forall m \in \text{pre}_j : i < j \wedge (\forall k : i \leq k < j \Rightarrow m \notin \text{post}_k) \Rightarrow$
   $\text{output}_{\Psi(\text{pre}_i, a_i, \text{post}_i)}(m) = \emptyset$

Let L be a regular language of Pre-Post-Pomsets over Σ_1 marked by Γ_1. A substitution Ψ is safe with respect to L if Ψ is safe with respect to π for all $\pi \in L$.

Example 6 (A Safe Substitution). Consider the Pre-Post-Pomsets π and π' defined in Examples 4 or 5, respectively.

Let Ψ a substitution such that $\Psi(\{a, b\}, e_2, \{c\}) = \pi$. Let us check the three conditions described in Definition 7 on Ψ. Notice that Ψ is only defined for $\pi'(2)$. Hence:

1. one has to check that $\forall m \notin \{a, b\}$: $\text{input}_\pi(m) = \emptyset$. Considering the set of marks $\Gamma_1 \cup \Gamma_2$, one can note that $\text{input}_\pi(1) = \text{input}_\pi(2) = \text{input}_\pi(c) = \emptyset$. Consequently, Condition 7 holds.
2. one has to check that $\forall m \in \{c\}$: $\text{output}_\pi(m) \neq \emptyset$. This is trivially true since, as shown in Example 4, $\text{output}_\pi(c) = \{e_3\}$. So, Condition 7 holds.
3. Since $[\pi'] = \{0, 1, 2, 3\}$, the initial condition can be reformulated into $\forall m \in \{c\}$: $(m \notin post_2) \implies \text{output}_\pi(m) = \emptyset$ where $post_2 = \{c\}$. Once again, considering the set of marks $\Gamma_1 \cup \Gamma_2$, $\text{output}_\pi(1) = \text{output}_\pi(2) = \text{output}_\pi(a) = \text{output}_\pi(b) = \emptyset$. So, Condition 7 holds.

Consequently, Ψ is a safe substitution.

Given a safe substitution Ψ and a Pre-Post-Pomset $\pi = (pre_0, a_0, post_0) \ldots (pre_n, a_n, post_n)$, the application of the substitution Ψ on π is denoted by $\Psi(\pi) = \Psi(pre_0, a_0, post_0) \ldots \Psi(pre_n, a_n, post_n)$. If Ψ is not defined for a given tuple $(pre_0, a_0, post_0)$, then the tuple remains the same. The following proposition explains the nature of the causality relations induced by a Pre-Post-Pomset resulting of the application of a safe substitution.

Proposition 3. *Let Ψ be a safe substitution from Pre-Post-Pomset over Σ_1 marked by Γ_1 to Pre-Post-Pomset over Σ_2 marked by Γ_2. Let π be a Pre-Post-Pomset over Σ_1 marked by Γ_1 such that $\pi = (pre_0, a_0, post_0) \cdots (pre_n, a_n, post_n)$. We denote by $l_0 \cdots l_n$ the Pre-Post-Pomset resulting from the application of Ψ on π, i.e. $\Psi(\pi)$, where $l_i = \Psi(pre_i, a_i, post_i) = (pre_{\tau(i,0)}, b_{\tau(i,0)}, post_{\tau(i,0)}) \cdots (pre_{\tau(i,k_i)}, b_{\tau(i,k_i)}, post_{\tau(i,k_i)})$ if Ψ is defined for the given tuple, $l_i = (pre_{\tau(i,0)}, b_{\tau(i,0)}, post_{\tau(i,0)}) = (pre_i, a_i, post_i)$ otherwise.*
Then for all positions $\tau(i_1, j_1)$, $\tau(i_2, j_2)$ in $\Psi(\pi)$, $\tau(i_1, j_1) \to \tau(i_2, j_2)$ iff one of two following conditions holds:

1. *$i_1 = i_2$ and $j_1 \to j_2$ in l_{i_1}*
2. *$i_1 < i_2, \exists m, i_1 \xrightarrow{m} i_2$ in $\pi \wedge j_1 \in \text{output}_{l_{i_1}}(m) \wedge j_2 \in \text{input}_{l_{i_2}}(m)$.*

Example 7. Let us illustrate the application of the safe substitution defined in Example 6. Considering $\pi = (\{a, b\}, e_0, \{1, 2\})(1, e_1, \emptyset)(2, e_2, \{c\})$ and $\pi' = (\emptyset, e'_0, a)$ $(\emptyset, e'_1, b)(\{a, b\}, e'_2, c)(c, e'_3, \emptyset)$, the application of the homomorphism Ψ on π' is:

$$\Psi(\pi') = (\emptyset, e'_0, a)(\emptyset, e'_1, b)\Psi(\{a, b\}, e'_2, c)(c, e'_3, \emptyset)$$
$$= (\emptyset, e'_0, a)(\emptyset, e'_1, b)\pi(c, e'_3, \emptyset)$$
$$= (\emptyset, e'_0, a)(\emptyset, e'_1, b)(\{a, b\}, e_0, \{1, 2\})(1, e_1, \emptyset)(2, e_2, \{c\})(c, e'_3, \emptyset).$$

The pomset $\textsf{toPomset}(\Psi(\pi'))$ is given Fig. 5. Let us check the causality relation Φ. From the word $\Psi(\pi')$, one can deduce that one has $\Phi(0, 2)$, $\Phi(1, 2)$, $\Phi(2, 3)$, $\Phi(2, 4)$ and $\Phi(4, 5)$ where $[\Psi(\pi')] = \{0, \ldots, 5\}$. Let us reformulate the positions $[\Psi(\pi')]$ according to the notations introduced in Proposition 3 i.e. $[\Psi(\pi')] = \{0, 1, 2, 3, 4, 5\} = \{\tau(0, 0), \tau(1, 0), \tau(2, 0), \tau(2, 1), \tau(2, 2), \tau(3, 0)\}$.

So, let us analyze the relation Φ:

1. $\Phi(0,2) \equiv \Phi(\tau(0,0), \tau(2,0))$. Condition 3 of Proposition 3 holds since $0 < 2$, $0 \xrightarrow{a} 2$ in π' and $0 \in \text{output}_{(\emptyset, e'_0, a)}(a)$ and $0 \in \text{input}_{(\{a,b\}, e_0, \{1,2\})}(a)$;
2. $\Phi(1,2) \equiv \Phi(\tau(1,0), \tau(2,0))$. Condition 3 of Proposition 3 holds since $1 < 2$, $1 \xrightarrow{b} 2$ in π' and $0 \in \text{output}_{(\emptyset, e'_1, b)}(b)$ and $0 \in \text{input}_{(\{a,b\}, e_0, \{1,2\})}(b)$;
3. $\Phi(2,3)$ and $\Phi(2,4)$: let us recall that $\Psi(\{a,b\}, e'_2, c) = \pi$. Consequently, one has $\Phi(\tau(2,0), \tau(2,1))$ and $\Phi(\tau(2,0), \tau(2,2))$. Condition 3 of Proposition 3 holds for both since these two relations are internal relations defined in π;
4. $\Phi(4,5) \equiv \Phi(\tau(2,2), \tau(3,0))$. Condition 3 of Proposition 3 holds since $2 < 3$, $2 \xrightarrow{c} 3$ in π' and $2 \in \text{output}_{\pi}(c)$ as well as $0 \in \text{input}_{(\{c\}, e'_3, \emptyset)}(c)$.

5   Modeling

In this section, we show that Pre-Post-Pomsets are expressive enough for the specification of classical concurrent system models i.e. synchronized products of transition systems in Sect. 5.1, Mazurkiewicz traces in Sect. 5.2 and parallel series in Sect. 5.3.

5.1   Synchronized Product

We now consider the matter of a synchronized product of systems as defined in [2, 20]. It is composed of a set of subsystems $(s_1, \cdots, s_n)$ on which we perform the same actions at the same time. Consequently, a subsystem may change its state after having executed the given action. In a synchronized product, a behavior is of the following form:

$$\sigma = (s^0_1, \cdots, s^0_n) \xrightarrow{a_0} (s^1_1, \cdots, s^1_n) \cdots (s^t_1, \cdots, s^t_n) \xrightarrow{a_t} (s^{t+1}_1, \cdots, s^{t+1}_n)$$

where s^t_j represents the state (configuration) of the subsystem s_j after having performed t actions.

To each action a_t, we associate a set $Act(a_t)$ representing the set of subsystems concerned by the given action. In order to define the pomset of a synchronized product behavior, we consider the notion of causal structure used in [2]. A behavior σ is formalized by the pomset $(E, \lambda, \rightarrow)$ where $E = \{(i,0) : i = 1 \ldots n\} \cup \{(i,t) : i \in Act(a_{t-1}) \wedge t > 0\}$, $\lambda(i,t) = s^t_i$ and $(i,t) \rightarrow (i',t')$ if $t > 0$, $t < t'$ and $i, i' \in Act(a_{t'-1})$.

In this structure, the set of events is can be seen as an history of changes on the subsystems, i.e. (i,t) where i is the identifier of the subsystem and t, a date. Thus, one can reconstruct a configuration from (i,t) using λ.

To encode such a structure with Pre-Post-Pomsets, each subsystem starts at date 0 without preconditions. This is represented in the left-hand side of the Pre-Post-Pomset π defined below, called *initial configurations*, and the right-hand side of the Pre-Post-Pomset in the same figure encodes the whole causality relation resulting from different actions at different times. The symbol $\prod$ denotes an iterative concatenation of words.

$$\pi = \underbrace{(\emptyset, s^0{}_1, 1) \cdots (\emptyset, s^0{}_n, n)}_{\text{Initial configurations}} \cdot \prod_{t>0} \left(\underbrace{(Act(a_{t-1}), \epsilon, Act(a_{t-1})) \prod_{i \in Act(a_{t-1})} (i, s^t{}_i, i)}_{t^{th} \text{ step}} \right)$$

Example 8 (A Pre-Post-Pomset for a synchronized product). Figure 6 describes two subsystems. They are composed of two states (A and B for the subsystem S1 and C and D for the subsystem S2). The actions u and v are respectively dedicated to subsystems S1 and S2. The action w has to be executed simultaneously by the two subsystems.

Figure 7 represents the graph of accessible states of the whole system. The synchronized action w implies that the two subsystems must change state simultaneously, while u and v involve local changes on each subsystem.

Let us consider the behavior of the whole system in Fig. 7:

$$\sigma = (A, C) \xrightarrow{u} (B, C) \xrightarrow{v} (B, D) \xrightarrow{w} (A, C) \cdots$$

Following the Pre-Post-Pomset construction given before Example 8, one can state that $a_0 = u$, $a_1 = v$, $a_2 = w$, ... From Fig. 6, one obtains $Act(a_0) = \{S1\}$, $Act(a_1) = \{S2\}$, $Act(a_2) = \{S1, S2\}$. Consequently, one can construct the Pre-Post-Pomset π as follows:

$$\pi = \underbrace{(\emptyset, A, 1) \cdot (\emptyset, C, 2)}_{\text{Initialization step}} \cdot \underbrace{((1, \epsilon, 1) \cdot (1, B, 1))}_{u \text{ execution}} \cdot \underbrace{((2, \epsilon, 2) \cdot (2, D, 2))}_{v \text{ execution}}$$

$$\cdot \underbrace{(((\{1, 2\}, \epsilon, \{1, 2\}) \cdot (1, A, 1) \cdot (2, C, 2))}_{w \text{ execution}} \cdots$$

The automaton of the Pre-Post-Pomsets is deduced from the graph of accessible states Fig. 7 by substituting each action by its translation and by prefixing the language by the translation of the initial configuration (see Fig. 8).

5.2 Mazurkiewicz Traces

A Mazurkiewicz trace [13] is defined by a couple (Σ, D) where Σ is the alphabet and D is a reflexive and symmetric dependence relation. The translation of a Mazurkiewicz trace σ to Pre-Post-Pomset is very simple. Let D_a be a set of letters such $D_a = \{b : (b, a) \in D\}$. Any trace $\sigma = a_0 \cdots a_i \cdots$ can be written as the Pre-Post-Pomset

$$\pi = (D_{a_0}, a_0, a_0) \cdots (D_{a_i}, a_i, a_i) \cdots . \tag{1}$$

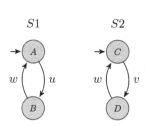

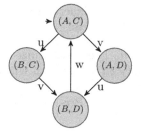

Fig. 6. Simple synchronized systems.   **Fig. 7.** Graph of accessible states.

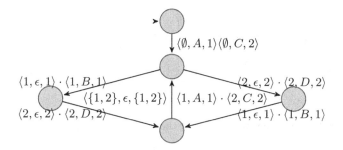

Fig. 8. Pre-Post-Pomset automaton of the synchronized product of Fig. 6.

Example 9. Let us consider the same study case than in Sect. 5.1, i.e. the system composed of two subsystems. Starting from the traces produced by the synchronized product of Fig. 7, we only focus on (observed) actions that are executed. Let $\sigma \in \{u, v, w\}^*$ be a word such that $\sigma = vuwuvw$ (corresponding to the two cycles of our subsystems). Let D be the dependencies defined such that $D = \{u, v, w\} \times \{u, v, w\} \setminus \{(u, v), (v, u)\}$. The trace over D represented by σ is $\{vuwuvw, vuwvuw, uvwuvw, uvwvuw\}$. Following the translation rule (1), one can construct the Pre-Post-Pomset π from σ and D as follows:

$$\pi = (D_u, u, u) \cdot (D_v, v, v) \cdot (D_w, w, w) \cdot (D_u, u, u) \cdot (D_v, v, v) \cdot (D_w, w, w)$$

with $D_u = \{u, w\}$, $D_v = \{v, w\}$ and $D_w = \{u, v, w\}$.

Figures 9 and 10 show the causality relations straight involved in each model. Note that, for a matter of clarity, reflexive relations do not appear in Fig. 10. However, recall that in terms of pomset, one has to consider the reflexive and transitive closures of the relation induced by the Pre-Post-Pomset. And in this

Fig. 9. Pomset induced by π.   **Fig. 10.** Dependency relation on σ.

context, we get exactly the same set of dependencies as one can find with Mazurkiewicz traces.

Example 10. The synchronized product of Example 8 can be considered as a Mazurkiewicz trace system when one wants to observe the actions. The dependance relation is $D = \{u, v, w\} \times \{u, v, w\} \setminus \{(u, v), (v, u)\}$. The result of the translation into a Pre-Post-Pomset language is given by the automaton Fig. 11.

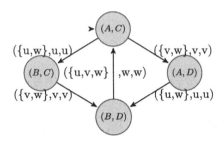

Fig. 11. Pre-Post-Pomset automaton of the Mazurkiewicz trace system of Fig. 6.

5.3 Parallel Series

Let a_i be events for $i \geq 0$. We define the set of parallel series expressions SP^{exp} as follows:

$$SP^{exp} = \begin{cases} \epsilon \in SP^{exp} \\ a_i \in SP^{exp} \\ t_1 \parallel t_2 \in SP^{exp} \text{ if } t_1, t_2 \in SP^{exp} \\ (t')^\omega \in SP^{exp} \quad \text{if } t' \in SP^{exp} \\ (t)^\parallel \in SP^{exp} \quad t \in SP^{exp} \\ (t)^* \in SP^{exp} \quad \text{if } t \in SP^{exp} \\ t_1 \cdot t_2 \in SP^{exp} \text{ if } t_1, t_2 \in SP^{exp} \end{cases}$$

Semantically speaking, $\parallel$ and $\cdot$ respectively specify the parallel execution and the sequential execution of actions. Consequently, for an action a, $(a)^\parallel$ specifies that a can be executed an unbounded number of times in parallel. Basically, such expressions may provide infinite pomsets.

Example 11. Let $e = a_0 \cdot (a_1)^\parallel \cdot a_2$ be a parallel series expression. Thus, an unbounded number of actions a_1 are executed in parallel. The corresponding pomset is given in Fig. 1.

In this section, we introduce the so-called to$^\Gamma$ function which transforms a parallel series expression into a Pre-Post-Pomset language encoding an equivalent set of pomsets. The function Op_f given Fig. 13 applies some operations on languages of Pre-Post-Pomsets into a single language of Pre-Post-Pomsets. Note that we use naturals as marks in the constructions proposed in Figs. 12

and 13. Moreover, $\circ$ denotes the composition of functions, i.e. $f \circ g(x) = f(g(x))$. In Fig. 13, considering L as a language of Pre-Post-Pomset of the form $L = (pre_0, a_0, post_0).L'.(pre_n, a_n, post_n)$, one has

- $in_i(L) = (i, a_0, post_0).L'.(pre_n, a_n, post_n)$ and
- $out_i(L) = (pre_0, a_0, post_0).L'.(pre_n, a_n, i)$.

Moreover, $inc_i(L)$ means that each mark j occurring at a *post* or a *pre* position is replaced by $i + j$.

Op_{op}	Result
$Op_.(p, p')$	$out_0(p).in_0(p')$
$Op_+(p, p')$	$p.p'$
$Op_*(p)$	$(\emptyset, \varepsilon, 0)p'^*(0, \varepsilon, \emptyset)$ with $p' = in_0 \circ out_0(p)$
$Op_\parallel(p)$	$(\emptyset, \varepsilon, \{0, 1, 2\}) \cdot L \cdot (\{0, 1, 2\}, \varepsilon, \emptyset)$ with $p' = in_2 \circ out_2 \circ inc_2(p)$ $L = \left((0, \varepsilon, \{0, 2\})p'(\{1, 2\}, \varepsilon, 1)\right)^*$
$Op_\parallel(p_1, p_2)$	$(\emptyset, \varepsilon, \{0, 2\}) \cdot L \cdot (\{1, 2\}, \varepsilon, \emptyset)$ with $f = in_2 \circ out_2 \circ inc_2$ and $L = f(p_1).(2, \epsilon, 1)(0, \epsilon, 2).f(p_2)$
$Op_\omega(p)$	$(\emptyset, \varepsilon, 0)in_0 \circ out_0(p)^\omega$

sp-expression	Result
$to^\Gamma(\varepsilon)$	$(\emptyset, \varepsilon, \emptyset)$
$to^\Gamma(a)$	$(\emptyset, a, \emptyset)$
$to^\Gamma(t \cdot t')$	$Op_.(to^\Gamma(t), to^\Gamma(t'))$
$to^\Gamma(t + t')$	$Op_+(to^\Gamma(t), to^\Gamma(t'))$
$to^\Gamma((t)^*)$	$Op_*(to^\Gamma(t))$
$to^\Gamma((t)^\parallel)$	$Op_\parallel(to^\Gamma(t))$
$to^\Gamma(t \parallel t')$	$Op_\parallel(to^\Gamma(t), to^\Gamma(t'))$
$to^\Gamma((t)^\omega)$	$Op_\omega(to^\Gamma(t))$

Fig. 12. Pre-Post-Pomset of parallel series expression.

Fig. 13. Operations on languages of Pre-Post-Pomsets.

This construction ensures that there exist a minimum and a maximum element in the pomset encoded by the generated Pre-Post-Pomset.

Example 12. Let e be the parallel series expression defined in Example 11. Let us apply to^Γ on e.

$$to^\Gamma(e) = Op_.(to^\Gamma(a_0), Op_.(Op_\parallel(to^\Gamma(a_1)), to^\Gamma(a_2)))$$

$$to^\Gamma(a_i) = (\emptyset, a_i, \emptyset) \text{ with } i \in \{0, 1, 2\} \tag{2}$$

$$Op_\parallel(to^\Gamma(a_1)) = Op_\parallel((\emptyset, a_1, \emptyset)) \tag{3}$$

$$= (\emptyset, \varepsilon, \{0, 1, 2\}) \cdot L \cdot (\{0, 1, 2\}, \varepsilon, \emptyset)$$

$$\text{with } L = \left((0, \varepsilon, \{0, 2\})(2, a_1, 2)(\{1, 2\}, \varepsilon, 1)\right)^*$$

$$Op_.((3), to^\Gamma(a_2)) = (\emptyset, \varepsilon, \{0, 1, 2\}) \cdot L \cdot (\{0, 1, 2\}, \varepsilon, 0)(0, a_2, \emptyset) \tag{4}$$

$$\text{with } L = \left((0, \varepsilon, \{0, 2\})(2, a_1, 2)(\{1, 2\}, \varepsilon, 1)\right)^*$$

$$Op_.((2), (4)) = (\emptyset, a_0, 0)(0, \varepsilon, \{0, 1, 2\}) \cdot L \cdot (\{0, 1, 2\}, \varepsilon, 0)(0, a_2, \emptyset) \tag{5}$$

$$\text{with } L = \left((0, \varepsilon, \{0, 2\})(2, a_1, 2)(\{1, 2\}, \varepsilon, 1)\right)^*$$

Altogether, $\mathsf{to}^\Gamma(e) = (\emptyset, a_0, 0)(0, \varepsilon, \{0, 1, 2\}) \cdot \Big((0, \varepsilon, \{0, 2\})(2, a_1, 2)(\{1, 2\}, \varepsilon, 1)\Big)^* \cdot (\{0, 1, 2\}, \varepsilon, 0)(0, a_2, \emptyset)$. Figure 2 illustrates the pomset encoded in $\mathsf{to}^\Gamma(e)$.

6 Conclusion

In this paper, we proposed a simple and expressive model for the specification of concurrent systems. Our contribution fits into the desire of a unified model well suited for the development of efficient verification tools in the domain of concurrent systems. We have also shown that the verification of MSO formula remains decidable. Undoubtedly, developing efficient tools will require a focus on fragments of logics, i.e. local logics [2,8,20]. These logics are extensions of LTL for the analysis of concurrent systems. Using our model, the verification problem of such logics remains probably PSPACE. Based on the following works [2,8,20], we could specify automata of elementary formulae of the local logics into Pre-Post-Pomsets and then study the complexity issues.

We also hope to adapt usual verification techniques such as symbolic verification or partial order reduction techniques. Moreover, our model and its composition operation make the study of different combinations of various models possible. For instance, one can combine synchronized products, parallel series or any new emerging models together as soon as these models are specifiable by Pre-Post-Pomsets.

Acknowledgments. We are immensely grateful to Anthony Perez for his comments on an earlier version of the manuscript.

References

1. Abadi, M., Lamport, L.: Composing specifications. ACM Trans. Program. Lang. Syst. **15**(1), 73–132 (1993)
2. Alur, R., Peled, D.A., Penczek, W.: Model-checking of causality properties. In: IEEE Symposium on Logic in Computer Science, pp. 90–100 (1995)
3. Alur, R., Peled, D.: Undecidability of partial order logics. Inf. Process. Lett. **69**(3), 137–143 (1999)
4. Arnold, A., Niwinski, D.: Rudiments of μ-Calculus. Elsevier, Amsterdam (2001)
5. Büchi, J.R.: On a decision method in restricted second order arithmetic. In: International Congress on Logic, Methodology and Philosophy of Science, pp. 1–11. Stanford University Press (1962)
6. Cheng, A.: Petri nets, traces, and local model checking. Theor. Comput. Sci. **183**(2), 229–251 (1997)
7. Courcelle, B., Engelfriet, J.: Graph Structure and Monadic Second-Order Logic: A Language-Theoretic Approach, 1st edn. Cambridge University Press, Cambridge (2012)
8. Gastin, P., Kuske, D.: Uniform satisfiability problem for local temporal logics over mazurkiewicz traces. Inf. Comput. **208**(7), 797–816 (2010)
9. Holzmann, G.J.: The SPIN Model Checker - Primer and Reference Manual. Addison-Wesley, Boston (2004)

10. Lamport, L.: The temporal logic of actions. ACM Trans. Program. Lang. Syst. **16**(3), 872–923 (1994)
11. Lodaya, K., Weil, P.: Series-parallel languages and the bounded-width property. Theor. Comput. Sci. **237**(1), 347–380 (2000)
12. Madhusudan, P.: Model-checking trace event structures. In: Logic in Computer Science, 2003, pp. 371–380. IEEE (2003)
13. Mazurkiewicz, A.: Concurrent program schemes and their interpretations. In: DAIMI Report Series **6**(78), July (1977)
14. McMillan, K.L.: Symbolic Model Checking. Kluwer Academic Publisher, Boston (1994)
15. Meenakshi, B., Ramanujam, R.: Reasoning about layered message passing systems. In: Verification, Model Checking, and Abstract Interpretation, pp. 268–282 (2003)
16. Mukund, M., Thiagarajan, P.S.: Linear time temporal logics over mazurkiewicz traces. In: Mathematical Foundations of Computer Science, pp. 62–92 (1996)
17. Muscholl, A., Peled, D.: Message sequence graphs and decision problems on mazurkiewicz traces. In: Kutylowski, M., Pacholski, L., Wierzbicki, T. (eds.) MFCS 1999. LNCS, vol. 1672, pp. 81–91. Springer, Heidelberg (1999). https://doi.org/10.1007/3-540-48340-3_8
18. Niebert, P., Huhn, M., Zennou, S., Lugiez, D.: Local first search — a new paradigm for partial order reductions. In: Larsen, K.G., Nielsen, M. (eds.) CONCUR 2001. LNCS, vol. 2154, pp. 396–410. Springer, Heidelberg (2001). https://doi.org/10.1007/3-540-44685-0_27
19. Nielsen, M., Plotkin, G., Winskel, G.: Petri nets, event structures and domains, part i. Theor. Comput. Sci. **13**(1), 85–108 (1981)
20. Ramanujam, R.: Locally linear time temporal logic. In: IEEE Symposium on Logic in Computer Science, pp. 118–127 (1996)
21. Thiagarajan, P.S., Henriksen, J.G.: Distributed versions of linear time temporal logic: a trace perspective. In: Reisig, W., Rozenberg, G. (eds.) ACPN 1996. LNCS, vol. 1491, pp. 643–681. Springer, Heidelberg (1998). https://doi.org/10.1007/3-540-65306-6_24
22. Thomas, W.: Languages, automata, and logic. In: Rozenberg, G., Salomaa, A. (eds.) Handbook of Formal Languages, pp. 389–455. Springer, Heidelberg (1997). https://doi.org/10.1007/978-3-642-59126-6_7
23. Weil, P.: Algebraic recognizability of languages. Math. Found. Comput. Sci. **3153**, 149–175 (2004)

Non-Standard Zeno-Free Simulation Semantics for Hybrid Dynamical Systems

Ayman Aljarbouh$^{(\boxtimes)}$ (iD)

Gipsa-lab, Grenoble INP, University of Grenoble Alpes, Grenoble, France
ayman.aljarbouh@univ-grenoble-alpes.fr

Abstract. Geometric-Zeno behavior is one of the most challenging problems in the analysis and simulation of hybrid systems. Geometric-Zeno solutions involve an accumulation of an infinite number of discrete events occurring in a finite amount of time. In models that exhibit geometric-Zeno, discrete events occur at an increasingly smaller distance in time, converging to a limit point according to a geometric series. In practice, simulating models of hybrid systems exhibiting geometric-Zeno is highly challenging, in that the simulation either halts or produces faulty results, as the time interval lengths are decreasing to arbitrary small positive numbers. Although many simulation tools for hybrid systems have been developed in the past years, none of them have a Zeno-free semantic model. All of them produce faulty results when simulating geometric-Zeno models. In this paper, we propose a non-standard Zeno-free mathematical formalism for detecting and eliminating geometric-Zeno during simulation. We derive sufficient conditions for the existence of geometric-Zeno behavior based on the existence of a non-standard contraction map in a complete metric space. We also provide methods for carrying solutions from pre-Zeno to post-Zeno. We illustrate the concepts with examples throughout the paper.

Keywords: Hybrid systems · Modeling and simulation · Zeno behavior · Simulation tools · Non-standard analysis · Model verification and completeness

1 Introduction

Hybrid systems are dynamical systems in which continuous and discrete dynamics interact with each other [15,22,35]. Such systems exist in a large number of technological systems, where the physical continuous evolution of the system is combined with embedded control actions [13,14]. Mathematical models of hybrid systems consist typically of continuous time dynamics—usually described by differential equations (or inclusions)—to describe the continuous behavior of the system, and discrete event dynamics, such as finite state machines that describe the discrete behavior of the system [12,19,22].

However, the interaction between the continuous and discrete dynamics of hybrid systems is complex in its nature, which necessitates a special attention

© Springer Nature Switzerland AG 2019
P. Ganty and M. Kaâniche (Eds.): VECoS 2019, LNCS 11847, pp. 16–31, 2019.
https://doi.org/10.1007/978-3-030-35092-5_2

from designers when using modeling abstraction (i.e. over-approximation) in building idealized models of hybrid systems. Intuitively, because of such modeling abstraction, the model jumps over instants corresponding to the violation of abstraction mechanisms. A bad use of modeling abstraction can lead to deviate models whose evolution is undefined at a certain point. One of these cases is the case of hybrid models that exhibit Zeno behavior. We define Zeno behavior as an infinite sequence of discrete events occurring in a finite amount of time.

We distinguish between two different types of Zeno behavior: (i) chattering-Zeno, and (ii) geometric-Zeno. In models that exhibit chattering-Zeno, the system infinitely moves back and forth between modes in a discrete fashion with infinitesimal time spent between the successive mode switchings [9–12]. In this paper, we focus on geometric-Zeno, which is defined as an accumulation of an infinite number of mode switchings that occur in finite time, where the solution of the model converges to a Zeno limit point according to a geometric series.

Geometric-Zeno behavior is one of the most challenging problems in the analysis and simulation of hybrid systems. In fact, simulation algorithms collapse if the solution of the simulated model is unspecified beyond a given point.

Many modeling and simulation tools for hybrid systems have been developed in the past years. They can be classified into two categories: (i) those who put special attention on defining models rigorously, such as for instance SpaceEx [26], Ptolemy [25] (based on the super-dense time semantics in [34]), and Zélus [21] (based on the non-standard semantics in [20]), and (ii) those who use informal approach for model definition such as Simulink [1], Modelica language [27] and its associated tools. The numerical solvers of these tools execute the continuous behavior by advancing time and computing the values of physical continuous variables. None of the above tools have a Zeno-free semantic model. They all rely on analyzing the solver output at each integration time step, with the solver behavior at the geometric-Zeno limit point being usually unspecified. As a result, the simulation halts, terminates with an error message, or becomes numerically incorrect and produces faulty results.

To deal with this problem, we propose, in this paper, a non-standard mathematical formalism for detecting and eliminating "orbitally" geometric-Zeno behavior during simulation. We derive sufficient conditions for the existence of geometric-Zeno behavior, and also we provide methods on how to allow for solutions to be carried beyond the geometric-Zeno point. The key idea of our approach is based on representing the hybrid solution trajectory as a non-standard sequence of hybrid states, and the convergence of such sequence to a geometric-Zeno limit point through a non-standard contraction map in a complete metric space. The existence of such non-standard contraction map indicates when a decision should be taken to transition the solution from pre-Zeno state to post-Zeno state, and thus eliminating geometric-Zeno behavior. We illustrate the methods with simulation results throughout the paper.

This paper is organized as follows: Sect. 2 discusses the related work. Section 3 introduces hybrid automata as a modeling formalism for hybrid systems. Section 4 presents a realistic case study of a hybrid system model having geometric-Zeno behavior, and discusses the challenges when simulating such model. Section 5 provides an analysis of geometric-Zeno behavior in a non-standard hybrid time domain. Section 6 presents methods for geometric-Zeno detection and elimination "on the fly" using non-standard analysis. Finally, we discuss the simulation results and summarize the contribution and the future work in Sects. 7 and 8, respectively.

2   Related Work

A technique that has been proposed to deal with Zeno is that of regularizing the original system, which was illustrated for particular examples in [17,24,30]. This technique is based on perturbing the dynamical system in order to obtain non-Zeno solution, and then taking the limit as the perturbation goes to zero. However, such perturbation may invalidate the notion of instantaneous discrete transitions. Consequently, this can result in models that are stiff, and as a result, the simulation performance might run into trouble.

Necessary and sufficient conditions for geometric-Zeno behavior in linear complementarity systems were provided in [23,36,37]. In the context of Lagrangian hybrid systems, Ames et al. have shown that geometric-Zeno limit points belong to the zero set of the unilateral switching function, with velocity vector being tangential to this switching surface [18]. Therefore, they postulated that after the Zeno time, the system switches to holonomically constrained dynamics, where the holonomic constraints are based on the unilateral constraints on the configuration space that originally defined the hybrid system.

In [31], Lamperski and Ames provided Lyapunov-like conditions for geometric-Zeno behavior in Lagrangian hybrid systems near isolated Zeno equilibrium points. The results in [31] were later extended in [28], where Zeno stability approach was described as a special form of asymptotic stability. Moreover, [28] provided Lyapunov conditions for Zeno stability of compact sets. More recently, the results of [31] were extended in [33] to Zeno equilibria that are non-isolated. Sufficient conditions for geometric-Zeno behavior in a special class of hybrid systems, called first quadrant hybrid systems were derived in [16]. This work was then generalized in [32] to set-valued first quadrant hybrid systems, with application to non-isolated Zeno equilibria in Lagrangian hybrid systems.

We observed that most of these proposed conditions for geometric-Zeno tend to be conservative, and apply to particular classes of hybrid systems, i.e. non-smooth mechanics, Lagrangian hybrid systems, first quadrant hybrid systems, linear complementarity systems, etc. We believe that this is because geometric-Zeno behavior is a global problem in its nature, which prevents the use of local methods in its regularization. While understanding geometric-Zeno in these domains is quite sophisticated, there is no proposition on how such methods can served in a hybrid semantic model design for modeling and simulation tools.

3   Hybrid Automata

Hybrid Automata is one of the main modeling formalisms used in hybrid systems theory. It is a transition system that is extended with continuous dynamics.

Definition 1 (Hybrid Automata). *A hybrid automaton $\mathcal{H}$ is a tuple $\mathcal{H} = (Q, X, Init, F, D, E, G, R)$, where:*

- $Q = \{q_i\}$, $i \in \mathbb{N}$, *is a finite set of discrete states or modes;*
- $X \subseteq \mathbb{R}^n$ *is the continuous state space ranged over by the state vector $x \in X$;*
- $Init \subset Q \times \mathbb{R}^n$ *is a finite set of states with initial conditions;*
- $F = \{f(q_i, x)\}$: $Q \times \mathbb{R}^n \to \mathbb{R}^n$ *is a set of vector fields, where for each $q_i \in Q$, the vector $\dot{x} = f(q_i, x)$ states the continuous evolution in $q_i \in Q$;*
- $D = \{Inv(q_i)\}$: $Q \to \mathbb{R}^n$ *is a set of invariants, where $Inv(q_i)$ is the domain of the vector $f(q_i, x)$. It restricts the continuous evolution within a location $q_i \in Q$ and specifies a set of admissible valuations for the continuous state;*
- $E = \{e_i\} \subseteq Q \times Q$, $i \in \mathbb{N}$, *is a set of discrete transitions, where each transition $e_i = (q_i, q_i') \in E$ determines the discrete successor state q_i' if the system is in a given discrete state q_i;*
- $G = \{\mathcal{G}(e_i)\}$: $E \to \mathbb{R}^n$ *is a finite set of guard conditions, where for each transition $e_i = (q_i, q_i') \in E$ there is a guard $\mathcal{G}(e_i) \in G$, which is a predicate over the continuous state variables in x;*
- $R = \{\mathcal{R}(e_i, x)\}$: $E \to \mathbb{R}^n \times \mathbb{R}^n$ *is a set of reset maps, where for each $e_i = (q_i, q_i') \in E$, the reset map $\mathcal{R}(e_i, x) \in R$ defines the new value that should be taken by the continuous state vector x during the transition $e_i \in E$.*

In the context of hybrid automata, the hybrid state (q_i, x) is a pair of a discrete state $q_i \in Q$ and a valuation $x \in \mathbb{R}^n$ of the continuous state variables.

Definition 2 (Hybrid Time Set). *A hybrid time set τ is a sequence of time intervals $\tau = \{I_i\}_{i=0}^N$ that is finite ($N < \infty$) or infinite ($N = \infty$) such that:*

- $I_i = [\tau_i, \tau_i']$ *for $0 \le i < N$;*
- *if $N < \infty$, then either $I_N = [\tau_N, \tau_N']$ or $I_N = [\tau_N, \tau_N')$ with $\tau_N' = \infty$; and*
- $\tau_i \le \tau_i' = \tau_{i+1}$ *for all i.*

The instants τ_i are times of discrete transitions. It is assumed that discrete transitions are instantaneous, therefore $\tau_i' = \tau_{i+1}$, where τ_i' corresponds to the time instant just before taking a discrete transition, whereas τ_{i+1} corresponds to the time instant just after taking a discrete transition.

Definition 3 (Hybrid Solution Trajectory). *A hybrid solution trajectory is a triple $\chi = (\tau, \{q_i\}_{i=0}^N, \{x_i = x(I_i)\}_{i=0}^N)$ consisting of a time set $\tau = \{I_i\}_{i=0}^N$ that is hybrid, and two sets of sequences represented by $q_i \in Q$ and $x_i : I_i \to \mathbb{R}^n$.*

Definition 4 (Hybrid Execution). *A hybrid solution trajectory is said to be an execution to a hybrid automaton $\mathcal{H}$ if it satisfies the following properties:*

- $(q_0, x_0) = (q_0, x_0(\tau_0)) \in Init$, *with $\tau_0 = 0$;*
- *for all $i < N$: $e = (q_i, q_{i+1}) \in E$, $x_i(\tau_i') \in \mathcal{G}(e)$, $x_{i+1}(\tau_{i+1}) \in \mathcal{R}(e, x_i(\tau_i'))$;*
- *for all i and all $t \in [\tau_i, \tau_i')$: $x_i(t) \in Inv(q_i)$, $\dot{x}_i(t) = f(q_i, x_i(t))$.*

4   Geometric-Zeno

In order to illustrate the problem of geometric-Zeno behavior, we give in the following a typical example of a hybrid system whose model exhibits geometric-Zeno behavior, and we discuss the challenges of simulating it.

Example (Two Tanks System). A canonical example of a geometric-Zeno model is the model of a water tanks system as sketched in Fig. 1. We denote x_1 and x_2 to the water levels, r_1 and r_2 to the critical thresholds, v_1 and v_2 to the constant water flow going out of the tanks, and w to the constant water flow going into either tank. We assume that $(v_1 + v_2) > w$. Thus, the water levels x_1 and x_2 keep dropping. When in either tanks the water level drops below the critical threshold, the pipe switches to deliver the water to that tank. Figure 2 shows the hybrid automaton model of the system, where switching the input water pipe between the two tanks occurs with zero time. With initial conditions $x_1(0) > r_1$ and $x_2(0) > r_2$, the water levels x_1 and x_2 will drop and as a result the input water pipe gets switched between the two tanks each time the water level hits the critical threshold in either tanks. As much and much water go out of tanks, we will see that the switching frequency of the input water pipe becomes higher and higher. In the limit point when $x_1(t) = r_1$ and $x_2(t) = r_2$, the switching frequency becomes infinite, and both guards $x_1(t) \leq r_1$ and $x_2(t) \leq r_2$ become instantaneously true. As a result, the hybrid automaton would not operate anymore in either of the modes q_1 and q_2.

Simulation tools get stuck when simulating this model. The numerical simulation of this example in Simulink, with the data set: $w = 1.8$, $v_1 = 1$, $v_2 = 1$, $r_1 = 5$, $r_2 = 5$, and $x(0) = [x_1(0) \; x_2(0)]^T = [8 \; 6]^T$, terminates with a halt at the Zeno time $t = 20.0018[sec]$. Other simulation tools give faulty simulation results when simulating geometric-Zeno models. It is the case of most of Modelica tools. For example, in simulating the above example in OpenModelica [2], when both x_1 and x_2 converge to the Zeno limit point $(x_1, x_2) = (r_1, r_2)$ at time $t = 20.0018[sec]$, the water level in one tank increases monotonically above the threshold, while the water level in the other tank decreases monotonically

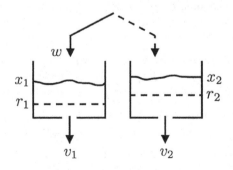

Fig. 1. Schematic of the two tanks system

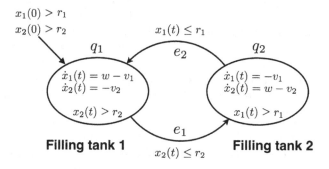

Fig. 2. The hybrid automaton of the two tanks model

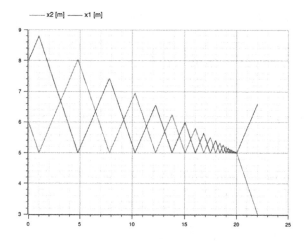

Fig. 3. Simulation of the two tanks model in OpenModelica

below the threshold (see Fig. 3). This is because discrete events are missed in the neighborhood of the geometric-Zeno limit point because of numerical errors due to the accumulation of an infinity of discrete transitions. Many other simulation tools, such as HyVisual [3], Scicos [4], Acumen [5], Zélus [6], give faulty results the same as in Modelica tools.

5   Non-Standard Analysis

Before introducing the non-standard hybrid time domain and the non-standard geometric-Zeno execution, we start first by giving a brief introduction to the theory of non-standard reals $^*\mathbb{R}$.

5.1   The Theory of Non-Standard Reals $^*\mathbb{R}$

The field $^*\mathbb{R}$ of non-standard reals has been used by several authors to define operational semantics of continuous and hybrid systems [20,21]. The idea is to enlarge the time domain by enlarging the standard reals numbers $\mathbb{R}$ and integers $\mathbb{N}$ into non-standard real numbers $*\mathbb{R}$ and non-standard $*\mathbb{N}$. The set of non-standard real number $*\mathbb{R}$ is constructed from the set of real number $\mathbb{R}$ via the ultra product [29].

We denote a non-standard object with the prefix $*$. For example, $*x$ denotes an element of $*\mathbb{R}$. Whenever we can obviously know that the object is non-standard, we omit the prefix $*$.

Definition 5 (Non-Standard Real Number). *We fix a free ultra filter $\mathcal{F}$ [29]. Let W denote a set of sequences of real numbers $(a_1, a_2, \cdots)$. A non-standard real number is defined by a set of sequences $\langle a_i \rangle_{i \in \mathbb{N}}$ closed under the following equivalence relation into W:*

$$\langle a_1, a_2, \cdots \rangle \sim \langle b_1, b_2, \cdots \rangle \Leftrightarrow \{k|\ a_k = b_k\} \in \mathcal{F}. \tag{1}$$

We denote the equivalence class of $(a_1, a_2, \cdots)$ by $[\langle a_1, a_2, \cdots \rangle]$. Namely, the non-standard real number is defined as the equivalence class $*\mathbb{R} = W/\sim$. We denote the set of non-standard numbers generated by integral sequences $\langle a_i \rangle_{i \in \mathbb{N}}$ with $a_i \in \mathbb{N}$ by $*\mathbb{N}$.

Every element of $\mathbb{R}$ is also an element of $*\mathbb{R}$ because for $x \in \mathbb{R}$ we have $[\langle x, x, \cdots \rangle] \in *\mathbb{R}$, namely, $\mathbb{R} \subseteq *\mathbb{R}$. By virtue of the ultra product construction of $*\mathbb{R}$, all properties of $\mathbb{R}$ also hold in $*\mathbb{R}$ (Transfer principle [20]).

Definition 6 (Infinitesimal, Infinite). *An infinitesimal $\partial \in *\mathbb{R}$ is a number of which absolute value is smaller than any non-zero standard real number. Namely, for all $a \neq 0 \in \mathbb{R}$ there exists an infinitesimal number $b \in *\mathbb{R}$ such that $|b| < |a|$. Infinite is a number of which absolute value is larger than any standard real number. Namely, for all $a \in \mathbb{R}$ there exists an infinite number $b \in *\mathbb{R}$ such that $|a| < |b|$.*

Definition 7 (Closeness). *We introduce a binary relation $a \approx b$ between two non-standard elements $a \in *\mathbb{R}$ and $b \in *\mathbb{R}$, which means that a is infinitesimally close to b. Namely, $a \approx b$ if and only if $|a - b|$ is infinitesimal.*

For any $x = [\langle x_1, x_2, \cdots \rangle] \in *\mathbb{R}$, we define a non-standard extension $*f(x)$ of a function $f(x)$ by $*f(x) = [\langle f(x_1), f(x_2), \cdots \rangle]$. The continuity of a standard function $*f(x)$ is described as follows: for all $x \in *\mathbb{R}$ there exists $y \in *\mathbb{R}$ such that $y \approx x$ and $*f(y) \approx *f(x)$.

5.2 Non-Standard Time Domain

The proposal in [20]—of defining the non-standard time domain—consists in defining the enlarged time set as

$$\mathbb{T}_\partial = \{t_n = n \times \partial|\ n \in *\mathbb{N}\}, \tag{2}$$

for a time base (which is infinitesimal) $\partial \in *\mathbb{R}, \partial > 0, \partial \approx 0$. This enlarged time set $\mathbb{T}_\partial$ contains large numbers as well.

It is possible, in fact, for any positive time $t_n \in \mathbb{T}_\partial$, to find a non-standard integer $n \in {}^*\mathbb{N}$ that satisfies $n \times \partial$ being greater than the time t_n. In [20], it was shown that this is due to the fact that the set of non-standard real numbers ${}^*\mathbb{R}$ is non-standard Archimedean.

In the following, we provide a formal definition to the non-standard execution of hybrid automata, as well as the formal definition to geometric-Zeno behavior in the non-standard hybrid time domain.

5.3   Non-Standard Geometric-Zeno Execution

The non-standard semantics of hybrid automata is based on using $\mathbb{T}_\partial$ as its time set for executing the hybrid automaton. It suffices in this context to keep the symbolic structure of the standard hybrid automata $\mathcal{H}$ (Definition 1) and only change the domain of interpretation of its execution from $\mathbb{R}$ to ${}^*\mathbb{R}$.

To ease for future discussion, we define a function $q(t)$ as the mode selector function that returns a discrete state in Q for any time instant t, that is, $q(t) = q_i \in Q$ for all t.

Definition 8 (Non-Standard Execution of $\mathcal{H}$). *Given a time base $\partial \in {}^*\mathbb{R}$, $\partial > 0$, $\partial \approx 0$, time index set $\mathbb{T}_\partial = \{t_n = n \times \partial|\ n \in {}^*\mathbb{N}\}$, and Boolean lattice $\mathbb{B}$. A non-standard execution ${}^*\chi$ of a hybrid automaton $\mathcal{H}$ is a tuple ${}^*\chi = (z(\cdot), q(\cdot), {}^*x(\cdot)) : \mathbb{T}_\partial \to \mathbb{B} \times Q \times {}^*\mathbb{R}^n$ defined as a finite or infinite sequence of infinitesimal iterations of states $(z, q, {}^*x) \in \mathbb{B} \times Q \times {}^*\mathbb{R}^n$ such that:*

1. *$(q(t_0), {}^*x(t_0)) \in {}^*Init$ and $z(0) = False$ when $t_0 = 0$;*
2. *ODE micro-step: For all $t \in \mathbb{T}_\partial$ such that ${}^*x(t) \in {}^*Inv(q(t))$: $z(t + \partial) = False$, $q(t + \partial) = q(t)$, ${}^*x(t + \partial) \in {}^*Inv(q(t + \partial))$, ${}^*x(t + \partial) = {}^*x(t) + \partial \times {}^*f(q(t), {}^*x(t))$;*
3. *Location change micro-step: For all $t \in \mathbb{T}_\partial$ such that $z(t + \partial) = True$: $q(t) = q_i$, $q(t + \partial) = q'_i$, ${}^*x(t) \in {}^*\mathcal{G}(e)$, $e = (q_i, q'_i) \in E$, and ${}^*x(t + \partial) \in {}^*\mathcal{R}(e, {}^*x(t))$.*

Whenever both invariants and guard conditions are simultaneously true then it is up to the modeler to give a priority either to the invariants or to guard conditions.

Definition 8 assumes priority is given to guard conditions whenever both invariants and guard conditions are simultaneously true. If priority is given to invariants, then location change micro-steps would be triggered when ${}^*x(t) \notin {}^*Inv(q(t))$.

Definition 9 (Non-Standard geometric-Zeno Execution). *A non-standard execution ${}^*\chi = (z(\cdot), q(\cdot), {}^*x(\cdot))$ of a hybrid automaton $\mathcal{H}$ is said to be non-standard geometric-Zeno execution at $t \in \mathbb{T}_\partial$ if and only if the sequence $\{t : z(t) = True\}$ is infinite for all $t \in [t_1, \partial, \{t\}, \partial, t_2] \subset \mathbb{T}_\partial$. This non-standard execution has a unique standard solution x given by $x = st({}^*x(\partial))$, where $st({}^*x(\partial))$ denotes the standardization of ${}^*x(\partial)$.*

6   Geometric-Zeno Detection and Elimination

A cyclic path is a prerequisite and a necessary condition for hybrid automata to accept geometric-Zeno executions. We consider that every pair of two consecutive triggers of the same guard as the input argument for detecting cycles.

The convergence of the execution of a hybrid automaton to a geometric-Zeno limit point is completely determined by the convergence of all the cycles detected during the execution through the discrete locations.

6.1   Cycles Detection

We firstly introduce the notion of simple cycles and finite cyclic paths in the finite directed graph (Q, E).

Definition 10 (Finite Cyclic Path). *Given a directed graph (Q, E), $E \subseteq Q \times Q$. A Finite cyclic path is an alternating sequence of discrete states $q_i \in Q$ and edges $e_i \in E$ of the form*

$$q_0 \xrightarrow{e_1} q_1 \xrightarrow{e_2} q_2 \xrightarrow{e_3} \cdots \xrightarrow{e_m} q_m$$

such that $e_i = (q_{i-1}, q_i)$ for all i. It is called a finite cyclic path if the starting state is the same as the ending state (i.e. $q_0 = q_m$). Also a portion of a finite path can be a finite cyclic path such as $q_1 \xrightarrow{e_2} q_2$ with $q_1 = q_2$, or $q_2 \xrightarrow{e_3} \cdots \xrightarrow{e_m} q_m$ with $q_2 = q_m$, etc.

We denote $C^{q_i} = \langle q_i; e_{i+1}, e_{i+2}, \cdots, e_m; q_i \rangle$ to a finite cyclic path with q_i being its starting and ending state, where $i \geq 0$ and both $m, i \in \mathbb{N}$ being finite. Furthermore, we denote $E(C^{q_i})$ to the set of all edges e_i that appear in the finite cyclic path C^{q_i}.

When applied to a finite cyclic path $C^{q_i} = \langle q_i; e_{i+1}, e_{i+2}, \cdots, e_m; q_m = q_i \rangle$, we get $E(C^{q_i}) = \{e_{i+1}, e_{i+2}, \cdots, e_m\}$.

During the execution of a hybrid automaton, a cycle is detected at τ_b on the finite cyclic path C^{q_i} if there exists a transition $e_k \in E(C^{q_i})$ such that

$$x(\tau_a) \in \mathcal{G}(e_k) \ \wedge \ x(\tau_b) \in \mathcal{G}(e_k), \quad \tau_a, \tau_b \in \tau, \quad \tau_b > \tau_a, \tag{3}$$

where τ is a sequence of intervals, $\mathcal{G}(e_k) \in G$ is the guard of the transition e_k. That is, a cycle is detected for every pair of two consecutive triggers of the same guard, within a non-zero duration.

Theorem 1 (Necessary Condition for Geometric-Zeno). *A hybrid automaton $\mathcal{H}$ can accept a geometric-Zeno execution only if there exists a finite cyclic path in the directed graph (Q, E) of $\mathcal{H}$.*

Proof. If (Q, E) has no cyclic path, then $\mathcal{H}$ accepts executions only with a finite number of discrete mode changes. Such an execution cannot be Zeno.

6.2 Geometric-Zeno Detection

We consider the evolution of the hybrid solution through cycles is represented as a transition system on a metric space. Therefore, in order to derive sufficient conditions for the hybrid automaton's execution to be convergent to a geometric-Zeno limit point, we study, based on non-standard analysis, the existence of a contraction map in a complete metric space, and the convergence of the solution to a geometric-Zeno point, through such map, as a Cauchy sequence.

Definition 11 (Non-Standard Euclidean Distance). *In Cartesian coordinates, consider two non-standard points* $^*p = (^*p_1, ^*p_2, \cdots, ^*p_n)$ *and* $^*q = (^*q_1, ^*q_2, \cdots, ^*q_n)$ *in a non-standard Euclidean n-space* $^*\mathbb{R}^n$. *The Euclidean distance* $d \in {}^*\mathbb{R}$ *between* $^*p$ *and* $^*q$ *is given by the Pythagorean formula by*

$$d(^*p, ^*q) = ||^*p, ^*q||_E = \sqrt{\sum_{i=1}^{n}(^*p_i - {}^*q_i)^2}. \tag{4}$$

Note that, in $^*\mathbb{R}$, *the distance between* $^*p_i$ *and* $^*q_i$ *is given by*

$$d(^*p_i, ^*q_i) = |^*p_i - {}^*q_i|. \tag{5}$$

Definition 12 (Non-Standard Metric Space). *A non-standard metric on a set* $^*X \subseteq {}^*\mathbb{R}^n$ *is a function* $d : {}^*X \times {}^*X \to {}^*\mathbb{R}$ *satisfying for* $^*x, ^*y, ^*z \in {}^*X$:

1. $d(^*x, ^*y) \geq 0$ *for all* $^*x, ^*y \in {}^*X$;
2. $d(^*x, ^*y) = 0$ *if and only if* $^*x = {}^*y$, *and* $d(^*x, ^*y) > 0$ *when* $^*x \neq {}^*y$;
3. $d(^*x, ^*y) = d(^*y, ^*x)$ *for all* $^*x, ^*y \in {}^*X$ *(Symmetry)*;
4. $d(^*x, ^*y) + d(^*y, ^*z) \geq d(^*x, ^*z)$ *for all* $^*x, ^*y, ^*z \in {}^*X$ *(Triangle Inequality)*.

A non-standard metric space is a pair $(^*X, d)$ *consisting of a set* $^*X \subseteq {}^*\mathbb{R}^n$ *and a non-standard metric* d *on* $^*X$.

Definition 13 (Open and Closed Balls and Sets in a Non-Standard Metric Space). *Given a non-standard metric space* $(^*X, d)$, *where* $^*X \subseteq {}^*\mathbb{R}^n$, *the open ball with center* $^*x \in {}^*X$ *and radius* $^*r$ *is the set*

$$^*B^o(^*x, ^*r) = \{^*y \in {}^*X : d(^*x, ^*y) < {}^*r\}. \tag{6}$$

A closed ball is defined analogously as the set

$$^*B^c(^*x, ^*r) = \{^*y \in {}^*X : d(^*x, ^*y) \leq {}^*r\}. \tag{7}$$

A subset $^*U$ *of a metric space* $(^*X, d)$ *is open if for all* $^*x \in {}^*U$, *there is* $^*r > 0$ *such that* $^*B^o(^*x, ^*r) \subset {}^*U$. *A subset* $^*U$ *of a metric space* $(^*X, d)$ *is closed if it complement* $^*X \setminus {}^*Y = \{^*x \in {}^*X | {}^*x \notin {}^*Y\}$ *is open. A subset* $^*U$ *of a metric space* $(^*X, d)$ *is bounded if there exists a closed ball of finite radius that contains it. That is,* $d(^*x, ^*y) \leq {}^*k$ *for all* $^*x, ^*y \in {}^*X$ *and some constant* $^*k < \infty$.

Definition 14 (Non-Standard Convergent Sequence). *In any set* $^*X$, *a sequence* $\{^*x_n\}$ *in* $^*X$ *is a mapping* $^*\rho : {}^*X \to {}^*X$, $n \mapsto {}^*x_n$, $n \in {}^*\mathbb{N}$. *Let* $(^*X, d)$ *be a metric space and* $\{^*x_n\} \subset {}^*X$, $n \in {}^*\mathbb{N}$, *be a sequence in* $^*X$, *we say that* $\{^*x_n\}$ *converges to an element* $^*x \in {}^*X$ *if for all* $\varepsilon > 0$, $\varepsilon \in {}^*\mathbb{R}$, *there exists* $N = N(\varepsilon) \in {}^*\mathbb{N}$ *such that for all* $n \geq N$, $d(^*x_n, {}^*x) < \varepsilon$. *We denote this by* $^*x_n \to {}^*x$, *and in this case,* $^*x$ *is said to be the limit of the sequence* $\{^*x_n\}$, *namely* $st(d(^*x_n, {}^*x)) \to 0$ *as* $n \to \infty$, *where* $st(d(\cdot))$ *denotes the standardization of* $d(\cdot)$. *If a sequence* $\{^*x_n\}$ *has a limit, then that limit is unique.*

Definition 15 (Non-Standard Cauchy Sequence). *Let* $(^*X, d)$ *be a metric space and* $\{^*x_n\} \subset {}^*X$, $n \in {}^*\mathbb{N}$, *be a sequence* $^*X$, *we say that* $\{^*x_n\}$ *is a Cauchy sequence if for all* $\varepsilon > 0$, $\varepsilon \in {}^*\mathbb{R}$, *there exists an* $N = N(\varepsilon) \in {}^*\mathbb{N}$ *such that for all* $m, n \geq N$, $m, n \in {}^*\mathbb{N}$, $d(^*x_n, {}^*x_m) < \varepsilon$. *As* $n, m \to \infty$ *we have* $st(d(^*x_n, {}^*x_m)) \to 0$.

Lemma 1. *A non-standard metric space* $(^*X, d)$ *is complete if every non-standard Cauchy sequence* $\{^*x_n\}$ *contained in* $^*X$ *is convergent to some* $^*x \in {}^*X$.

Definition 16 (Non-Standard Contraction Mapping in Non-Standard Metric Space). *Let* $^*\rho : {}^*X \to {}^*X$ *be a non-standard map on the non-standard metric space* $(^*X, d)$. *We say that* $^*\rho$ *is a contraction of modulus* $\beta \in {}^*\mathbb{R}$ *if there exists* $\beta \in (0, 1)$, $\beta \in {}^*\mathbb{R}$, *such that* $d(^*\rho(^*x), {}^*\rho(^*y)) \leq \beta d(^*x, {}^*y)$ *for all* $^*x, {}^*y \in {}^*X$. *Informally, a contraction map brings any two points of a set closer to each other.*

Theorem 2. *Let* $(^*X, d)$ *be a non-standard complete metric space and* $^*\rho : {}^*X \to {}^*X$ *be a non-standard contraction map, then:*

1. $^*\rho$ *has a unique fixed point; that is there exists a unique* $^*x^* \in {}^*X$ *with* $^*\rho(^*x) = {}^*x^*$,
2. *the sequence* $^*x_1 = {}^*\rho(^*x_0)$, $^*x_2 = {}^*\rho(^*x_1)$, ..., $^*x_{n+1} = {}^*\rho(^*x_n)$ *is a Cauchy sequence in* $^*X$, *and converges to* $^*x^*$ *for any starting point* $^*x_0 \in {}^*X$.

Proof. Pick any $^*x_1 \in {}^*X$ and iterate $^*x_{n+1} = {}^*\rho(^*x_n)$, $n = 1, 2, \cdots$. For all n we have

$$d(^*x_{n+1}, {}^*x_n) \leq \beta^{n-1} d(^*x_2, {}^*x_1), \tag{8}$$

noting that

$$d(^*x_{n+2}, {}^*x_{n+1}) = d(^*\rho(^*x_{n+1}), {}^*\rho(^*x_n)) \leq \beta d(^*x_{n+1}, {}^*x_n). \tag{9}$$

If $m > n$ we deduce that

$$d(^*x_m, {}^*x_n) \leq \beta^{n-1}(1 + \cdots + \beta^{m-n-1}) d(^*x_2, {}^*x_1), \tag{10}$$

$$d(^*x_m, {}^*x_n) \leq \frac{\beta^{n-1}}{1 - \beta} d(^*x_2, {}^*x_1). \tag{11}$$

Hence $\{^*x_n\}$ is a Cauchy sequence, and since $^*X$ is complete then $^*x_n \to {}^*x^*$ for some $^*x^* \in {}^*X$. Passing to the limit in $^*x_{n+1} = {}^*\rho(^*x_n)$ we get $^*x^* = {}^*\rho(^*x^*)$, so that $^*x^*$ is a fixed point.

Theorem 3 (Sufficient Condition for Geometric-Zeno Behavior). *An execution of a hybrid automaton* $\mathcal{H}$ *is geometric-Zeno if the following two conditions are satisfied:*

1. *The directed graph* $(\mathcal{Q}, E)$ *of* $\mathcal{H}$ *contains at least one finite cyclic path, i.e. the necessary condition is fulfilled.*
2. *The hybrid solution trajectory is a non-standard Cauchy sequence* $\{^*x_n\}$, $n \in {}^*\mathbb{N}$, *in a complete non-standard metric space* $^*X$. *Any line that starts from the limit* $^*x^*$ *of* $\{^*x_n\}$ *and intersects all cycles will form a non-standard Cauchy subsequence* $\{^*x_j\} \subset \{^*x_n\}$, $j \in {}^*\mathbb{N}$, *satisfying* $^*x_{j+1} = {}^*\rho(^*x_j)$ *for all* j, *with* $^*\rho$ *being non-standard contraction map of fixed modulus* β. *The limit point to which both Cauchy sequences* $\{^*x_n\}$ *and* $\{^*x_j\}$ *converge is the geometric-Zeno limit point.*

6.3   Geometric-Zeno Elimination

A way to eliminate geometric-Zeno behavior is by stopping the Cauchy sequence $\{^*x_n\}$ of the solution at $^*x_n \in \{^*x_n\}$ once $^*x_n \approx {}^*\rho(^*x_n)$. The step in which $^*x_n \approx {}^*\rho(^*x_n)$ would be used to transition the solution from pre-Zeno to post-Zeno. The idea of carrying the execution beyond the geometric-Zeno limit point is by forcing the system to slide at the geometric-Zeno limit point. When the transition from pre-Zeno to post-Zeno is taken, the systems switches to the sliding dynamics $^*f_\infty = 0 \cdot {}^*f(q_i, {}^*x)$ where $^*f(q_i, {}^*x)$ is the original dynamics of the system. The transition from pre-Zeno to post-Zeno is urgent. When the transition from pre-Zeno to post-Zeno is taken, the rest of the events before the geometric-Zeno point are discarded.

7   Simulation Results

As a simulation environment for the prototype implementation of our proposed technique we have used Matlab/Simulink simulation tool. We have implemented two Zeno-free simulators in both Matlab and Simulink environments. The motivation is show the applicability of our proposed methods. The Matlab implementation [7] includes a stand-alone Zeno-free simulator written in Matlab code, while the Simulink implementation [8] includes the basic Simulink library blocks that allow for Zeno-free simulation of Zeno models written in Simulink.

Figure 4 shows the Zeno-free simulation results for the two tanks system presented in Sect. 4 with the data set: $w = 1.8$, $v_1 = 1$, $v_2 = 1$, $r_1 = 5$, $r_2 = 5$, and $x(0) = [x_1(0)\ x_2(0)]^T = [8\ 6]^T$. The simulation time is set to 25 [sec].

Two cyclic paths, $C^{q_1} = \langle q_1; e_1, e_2; q_1 \rangle$ and $C^{q_2} = \langle q_2; e_2, e_1; q_2 \rangle$, were detected by the simulator when executing the hybrid automaton of the system, where e_1 is the transition from q_1 to q_2 guarded by the guard $\mathcal{G}(e_1) = \{x(t) \in \mathbb{R}^2 : x_2(t) \leq r_2\}$, and e_2 is the transition from q_2 to q_1 guarded by the guard $\mathcal{G}(e_2) = \{x(t) \in \mathbb{R}^2 : x_1(t) \leq r_1\}$. The initial cycle on the cyclic path $C^{q_1} = \langle q_1; e_1, e_2; q_1 \rangle$ was detected at the time instant $t = 7.8402$, and the initial

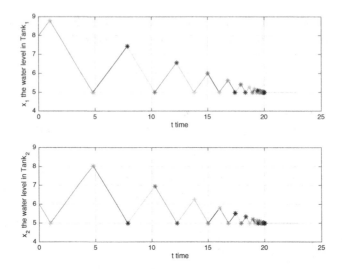

Fig. 4. Zeno-free simulation of the two tanks model. Up: The time evolution of x_1. Down: The time evolution of x_2.

cycle on the cyclic path $C^{q_2} = \langle q_2; e_2, e_1; q_2 \rangle$ was detected at the time instant $t = 10.2723$. The convergence of solution to the Zeno limit point was estimated to be at time 20.0018. The dense points near the Zeno time 20.0018 indicates that more and more computation steps were taken near the Zeno limit point. The simulation closely approaches the geometric-Zeno point before the simulator automatically switches to integrate the system with the sliding dynamics $(\dot{x}_1(t) = 0, \dot{x}_2(t) = 0)$, (i.e. sliding along the surface to which belong the Zeno state $x_\infty = \{x(t) \in \mathbb{R}^2 : x_1(t) = r_1 \wedge x_2(t) = r_2\}$, carrying the solution past the geometric-Zeno limit point.

8   Conclusion and Perspectives

In this paper, we addressed the problem of geometric-Zeno behaviors of hybrid systems. We provided an analysis for geometric-Zeno executions in a nonstandard *densely ordered* hybrid time domain. The advantages of using nonstandard semantics in the analysis of geometric-Zeno behavior is that the completeness in the space of the continuous dynamics and discrete dynamics is naturally introduced, so that it allows representing geometric-Zeno solutions in a concrete way, while at the same time preserving the original semantics of the model. We also proposed a Zeno-free mathematical formalism for simulation semantics in the purpose of allowing for simulation tools an efficient detection and elimination of geometric-Zeno. We formally introduced conditions on when the simulated hybrid models exhibit geometric-Zeno. We also provided methods for carrying solution beyond geometric-Zeno limit point. A part of the work was attributed to design, test, and validate Zeno-free prototype implementations using the proposed methods.

The work presented in this paper can be continued in many different directions. A future research direction would be to discuss how the methods proposed in this paper would be used in a mixed hybrid simulation technique combining event-driven simulation and time-stepping simulation. Another future research direction would be to explore our methods in experimental case studies of complex hybrid systems having a large number of state variables, and whose models exhibit geometric-Zeno behavior.

Acknowledgements. This work is supported by the European project ITEA3 MODRIO under contract N° 6892, and the Grant ARED of Brittany Regional Council.

References

1. https://www.mathworks.com/products/simulink.html
2. https://openmodelica.org/
3. https://ptolemy.berkeley.edu/hyvisual/
4. http://www.scicos.org/
5. http://www.acumen-language.org/
6. http://zelus.di.ens.fr/
7. DOMNA: a lite matlab simulator for zeno-free simulation of hybrid dynamical systems, with zeno detection and avoidance in run-time. https://bil.inria.fr/fr/software/view/2691/tab
8. Sevama: A simulink toolbox and simulator for zeno-free simulation of hybrid dynamical systems, with zeno detection and avoidance in run-time. https://bil.inria.fr/fr/software/view/2679/tab
9. Aljarbouh, A., Caillaudr, B.: Simulation for hybrid systems: chattering path avoidance. In: Proceedings of the 56th Conference on Simulation and Modelling (SIMS 56), Linkoping Electronic Conference Proceedings, vol. 119, pp. 175–185 (2015). https://doi.org/10.3384/ecp15119175
10. Aljarbouh, A., Caillaudr, B.: Chattering-free simulation of hybrid dynamical systems with the functional mock-up interface 2.0. In: Proceedings of the First Japanese Modelica Conferences, Linkoping Electronic Conference Proceedings, vol. 124, pp. 95–105 (2016). https://doi.org/10.3384/ecp1612495
11. Aljarbouh, A., Zeng, Y., Duracz, A., Caillaud, B., Taha, W.: Chattering-free simulation for hybrid dynamical systems semantics and prototype implementation. In: 2016 IEEE International Conference on Computational Science and Engineering (CSE) and IEEE International Conference on Embedded and Ubiquitous Computing (EUC) and 15th International Symposium on Distributed Computing and Applications for Business Engineering (DCABES), pp. 412–422, August 2016. https://doi.org/10.1109/CSE-EUC-DCABES.2016.217
12. Aljarbouh, A., Caillaud, B.: On the regularization of chattering executions in real time simulation of hybrid systems. In: Cap, C. (ed.) Baltic Young Scientists Conference, p. 49. The 11th Baltic Young Scientists Conference, Universität Rostock, Tallinn, Estonia, July 2015. https://hal.archives-ouvertes.fr/hal-01246853
13. Alur, R., et al.: Hybrid systems the algorithmic analysis of hybrid systems. Theor. Comput. Sci. **138**(1), 3–34 (1995). https://doi.org/10.1016/0304-3975(94)00202-T. http://www.sciencedirect.com/science/article/pii/030439759400202T

14. Alur, R., Henzinger, T.A., Ho, P.H.: Automatic symbolic verification of embedded systems. IEEE Trans. Softw. Eng. **22**(3), 181–201 (1996). https://doi.org/10.1109/32.489079
15. Alur, R., Henzinger, T.A.: Modularity for timed and hybrid systems. In: Mazurkiewicz, A., Winkowski, J. (eds.) CONCUR 1997. LNCS, vol. 1243, pp. 74–88. Springer, Heidelberg (1997). https://doi.org/10.1007/3-540-63141-0_6
16. Ames, A.D., Abate, A., Sastry, S.: Sufficient conditions for the existence of zeno behavior. In: Proceedings of the 44th IEEE Conference on Decision and Control, pp. 696–701, December 2005. https://doi.org/10.1109/CDC.2005.1582237
17. Ames, A.D., Sastry, S.: Blowing up affine hybrid systems. In: 43rd IEEE Conference on Decision and Control, CDC, vol. 1, pp. 473–478, December 2004. https://doi.org/10.1109/CDC.2004.1428675
18. Ames, A.D., Zheng, H., Gregg, R.D., Sastry, S.: Is there life after zeno? Taking executions past the breaking (zeno) point. In: 2006 American Control Conference, 6 pp., June 2006. https://doi.org/10.1109/ACC.2006.1656623
19. Antsaklis, P.J.: Special issue on hybrid systems: theory and applications a brief introduction to the theory and applications of hybrid systems. Proc. IEEE **88**(7), 879–887 (2000). https://doi.org/10.1109/JPROC.2000.871299
20. Benveniste, A., Bourke, T., Caillaud, B., Pouzet, M.: Non-standard semantics of hybrid systems modelers. J. Comput. Syst. Sci. **78**(3), 877–910 (2012). http://www.sciencedirect.com/science/article/pii/S0022000011001061. In Commemoration of Amir Pnueli
21. Bourke, T., Pouzet, M.: Zélus: a synchronous language with ODEs. In: Belta, C., Ivančić, F. (eds.) HSCC - Proceedings of the 16th International Conference on Hybrid Systems: Computation and Control, pp. 113–118, Calin Belta and Franjo Ivančić. ACM, Philadelphia, April 2013. https://doi.org/10.1145/2461328.2461348. https://hal.inria.fr/hal-00909029
22. Cai, C., Goebel, R., Sanfelice, R.G., Teel, A.R.: Hybrid systems: limit sets and zero dynamics with a view toward output regulation. In: Astolfi, A., Marconi, L. (eds.) Analysis and Design of Nonlinear Control Systems, pp. 241–261. Springer, Heidelberg (2008). https://doi.org/10.1007/978-3-540-74358-3_15
23. Camlibel, M.K., Schumacher, J.M.: On the zeno behavior of linear complementarity systems. In: Proceedings of the 40th IEEE Conference on Decision and Control, vol. 124, pp. 346–351 (2001). https://doi.org/10.1109/.2001.980124
24. Egerstedt, M., Johansson, K.H., Sastry, S., Lygeros, J.: On the regularization of Zeno hybrid automata. Syst. Control. Lett. **38**, 141–150 (1999). https://control.ee.ethz.ch/index.cgi?page=publications;action=details;id=2985
25. Eker, J., Janneck, J.W., Lee, E.A., Ludvig, J., Neuendorffer, S., Sachs, S.: Taming heterogeneity - the ptolemy approach. Proc. IEEE **91**(1), 127–144 (2003). https://doi.org/10.1109/JPROC.2002.805829
26. Frehse, G., et al.: SpaceEx: scalable verification of hybrid systems. In: Gopalakrishnan, G., Qadeer, S. (eds.) CAV 2011. LNCS, vol. 6806, pp. 379–395. Springer, Heidelberg (2011). https://doi.org/10.1007/978-3-642-22110-1_30
27. Fritzson, P.: Introduction to Modeling and Simulation of Technical and Physical Systems with Modelica. Wiley-IEEE Press, Hoboken (2011)
28. Goebel, R., Teel, A.R.: Lyapunov characterization of zeno behavior in hybrid systems. In: 47th IEEE Conference on Decision and Control, CDC 2008, pp. 2752–2757, December 2008. https://doi.org/10.1109/CDC.2008.4738864
29. Goldblatt, R.: Lecture on the Hyperreals: An Introduction to Nonstandard Analysis. Springer, Heidelberg (1988)

30. Johansson, K.H., Lygeros, J., Sastry, S., Egerstedt, M.: Simulation of zeno hybrid automata. In: Proceedings of the 38th IEEE Conference on Decision and Control, vol. 4, pp. 3538–3543 (1999). https://doi.org/10.1109/CDC.1999.827900
31. Lamperski, A., Ames, A.D.: Lyapunov-like conditions for the existence of zeno behavior in hybrid and Lagrangian hybrid systems. In: 2007 46th IEEE Conference on Decision and Control, pp. 115–120, December 2007. https://doi.org/10.1109/CDC.2007.4435003
32. Lamperski, A., Ames, A.D.: On the existence of zeno behavior in hybrid systems with non-isolated zeno equilibria. In: 47th IEEE Conference on Decision and Control, CDC 2008, pp. 2776–2781, December 2008. https://doi.org/10.1109/CDC.2008.4739100
33. Lamperski, A., Ames, A.D.: Lyapunov theory for zeno stability. IEEE Trans. Autom. Control **58**(1), 100–112 (2013). https://doi.org/10.1109/TAC.2012.2208292
34. Lee, E.A., Zheng, H.: Operational semantics of hybrid systems. In: Morari, M., Thiele, L. (eds.) HSCC 2005. LNCS, vol. 3414, pp. 25–53. Springer, Heidelberg (2005). https://doi.org/10.1007/978-3-540-31954-2_2
35. Lygeros, J., Tomlin, C., Sastry, S.: Hybrid systems: modeling, analysis and control. Lecture Notes on Hybrid Systems (2008). http://www-inst.cs.berkeley.edu/~ee291e/sp09/handouts/book.pdf
36. Shen, J., Pang, J.S.: Linear complementarity systems: zeno states. SIAM J. Control Optim. **44**(3), 1040–1066 (2005). https://doi.org/10.1137/040612270, http://dx.doi.org/10.1137/040612270
37. Thuan, L.Q.: Non-zenoness of piecewise affine dynamical systems and affine complementarity systems with inputs. Control Theory Technol. **12**(1), 35–47 (2014). https://doi.org/10.1007/s11768-014-0074-5. http://dx.doi.org/10.1007/s11768-014-0074-5

Static Detection of Event-Driven Races in HTML5-Based Mobile Apps

Phi Tuong Lau[✉]

Faculty of Computer Engineering, University of Information Technology,
Ho Chi Minh City, Vietnam
laulpt@gmail.com

Abstract. HTML5-based mobile apps are developed using standard web technologies such as HTML5, CSS, JavaScript, so they may also face with event-based races as web apps. The races in such mobile apps can be caused by various sources of asynchronous events, especially, middlware framework events. For example, PhoneGap framework supports the lifecycle events for signaling states of an app like Android's lifecycle and the resource access events for interacting with the platform resources such as contact, SMS, etc. When those events fire, it may generate nondeterministic execution orders of corresponding event handlers. Those nondeterminisms may raise data races among them.

In this paper, we introduce event-based races in HTML5-based mobile apps. Moreover, we propose a semi-automated approach combining static data flow analysis with manual code inspection for race detection. To evaluate it, we ran our proposed approach on a dataset of 1,926 HTML5-based mobile apps for detecting event-based races. Eventually, it scanned out totally 18 vulnerable apps. We manually inspected such vulnerable apps and discovered out 21 true races.

Keywords: HTML5-based mobile app · PhoneGap · Event-driven race · Data flow analysis · Happens-before · Concurrency

1 Introduction

HTML5-based mobile apps are increasing their popularity due to their advantages for reducing costs in process development compared with native mobile apps. Since they leverage standard web technologies to simply be ported on various platforms and an event-driven programming model, so they may be subject to face with event-driven races as web apps.

Event-based races are common sources of errors in JavaScript-based web apps and can occur by triggering user events, system events, and network events asynchronously. For example, a user event is fired by clicking on a button. As a response to the user event, a web browser invokes a JavaScript function defined as its event handler in a web page. A race can find out when the user clicks on the button before or after its event handler is loaded from a JavaScript file. If it is clicked before loading its event handler, then the user event is lost since the event handler has not yet registered.

© Springer Nature Switzerland AG 2019
P. Ganty and M. Kaâniche (Eds.): VECoS 2019, LNCS 11847, pp. 32–46, 2019.
https://doi.org/10.1007/978-3-030-35092-5_3

On the other hand, event-driven races can be found in HTML5-based mobile apps from various sources of asynchronous events. First, the races can be caused by system events, user events, network events like web apps. In addition, they may occur once middleware framework events fire. A middleware framework provides a vast variety of asynchronous events for building hybrid mobile apps in a real-time manner. For example, PhoneGap framework is integrated with the lifecycle events used for saving and restoring states of an app like Android's lifecycle and the events used in interaction with the platform resources such as contact, SMS, etc. We consider such type of the events as resource access events. When these events fire asynchronously, it may create unexpected execution orders of the corresponding event handlers. Those nondeterminisms may raise data races among the events.

The previous work introduced different approaches to detect event-based races in web apps [1–9]. Hong et al. [1] implemented a testing framework to detect concurrency bugs. Jensen et al. [5] applied test execution for detecting the races. Adamsen et al. [3] leveraged dynamic instrumentation combining with test execution for identifying AJAX-based races. Madsen et al. [6] analyzed specific types of errors raised by event-based races in Node.js programs. Most of those work considered the races occured by user events, system events, and network events. Additionally, event-based races are also found in native mobile apps, especially, Android apps [15–18, 20]. Hu et al. [15] and Bielik et al. [16] employed static program analysis for detecting the races in Android apps. Tang et al. [19] applied automated test generation for finding out concurrency bugs. Those researchers aimed at detecting the races resulting from firing the Android framework events, user actions, Android threads, etc.

Our work. We propose a semi-automated approach by combining the static data flow analysis with the manual code inspection to scan event-based races in HTML5-based mobile apps. Comparing with the previous researches, our work targets to the races raised by the asynchronous events of a middleware framework. We select the asynchronous events of PhoneGap framework because of its popularity. Our proposed approach is designed by the following steps.

In the first step, it executes event traces to slice API calls for registering/triggering the asynchronous events in a given app. Comparing with the related work, they leveraged dynamic instrumentation [1, 3, 5, 8], static analysis [15–18, 20] to collect sequences of operations in apps as event traces. In fact, it is mostly impossible to trace all sequences of operations in large-scale JavaScript programs due to its highly dynamic features. Such API calls collected are then put into a list of pairs so that each pair consists of two API calls based on the principle of combinations in mathematic.

In the second step, it finds out vulnerable pairs from the list of the pairs. The related approaches are basically extended from conventional analysis techniques such as vector clocks, modeling happens-before rules [15–18] for tracking happens-before relationship in sequences of events. We implemented the data flow analysis to identify happens-before relations between two API calls in each pair based on a happens-before rule. The rule is defined that when the event handlers of two API calls are nested, there does exist happens-before relations between them. Otherwise, they could be concurrently executed. In this case, it checks whether the event handlers of them access to the same memory locations. If so, it will flag the pair as a vulnerable pair.

The vulnerable pairs may not cause harmful races. To detect true races, we conduct additionally the manual code analysis for the vulnerable pairs by manually generating possible schedules of the events from each pair. We manually verify whether there does exist any schedule that can cause data conflicts between the events.

Evaluation. We downloaded a dataset of 1,926 HTML5-based mobile apps from Google Play Stores and other third-party stores. We carried out our approach to analyze the dataset. As a result, it scanned out 18 vulnerable apps consisting of 23 vulnerable pairs. Then, we conducted a manual code review of such 23 vulnerable pairs and found out 21 true data races among events. Such races fit into the following categories: 9 data races caused by database transactions, 3 data races by file system requests, 5 data races caused by the lifecycle events, and 4 data races occurring as accessing to the contact of a mobile device.

Main contribution. We make the academic contributions as follows.

- We describe event-based races in HTML5-based mobile apps.
- We propose a semi-automated approach combining the data flow analysis with the manual code inspection for detecting the event-based races.
- We show the evaluation on a dataset of 1,926 HTML5-based mobile apps. Eventually, we manually figured out 21 true races from 18 vulnerable apps.

The structure of this paper is organized as follows. Section 2 presents background. Section 3 presents our motivation. Section 4 describes asynchronous middleware framework events. Section 5 describes our methodology. Section 6 shows the evaluation of our proposed approach. Section 7 reviews the related work. Section 8 concludes this research.

2   Background

2.1 Middleware Framework

A middleware framework is integrated as a communication bridge between a mobile web browser (e.g. WebView) and the native system features such as camera, contact, SMS, etc. in hybrid mobile apps or so called HTML5-bassed mobile apps. There are some well-known middleware frameworks such as PhoneGap (Cordova) [38], Ionic [39], Framework 7 [40], etc. that are developed for building such mobile apps. Those frameworks are powerful and have their own capabilities.

In this paper, we pick up PhoneGap because of the possible reasons as follows. First of all, it supports for well-known platforms such as Android, iOS, etc. Second, Most of PhoneGap APIs are asynchronous [41], so when the APIs are executed, their event handlers as callback functions can be dispatched nonderministically. Second, it was used in the related researches [27, 29, 32]. Last but not least, it is integrated as the core of other popular frameworks such as Ionic [39], Framework 7 [40], and so on. The architecture of an HTML5-based mobile app includes native code (e.g. Java) for accessing the native system functionalities such as camera, contact, etc., and a powerful web browser (e.g. WebView in Android) using standard web technologies.

2.2 Event-Based System

Event-based systems are often used when either an action or an occurrence is asynchronously fired by external activities and internal alarms which need to be handled. For example, a user action as clicking on a mouse, or an occurrence as task timeout.

Event-based programming can cause concurrency bugs as standard multi-threaded programming such as C, Java. Event handlers resulting from firing events are scheduled by a dispatcher. The event-based programing is often executed in a single thread atomically, so the programs cannot be concurrently executed, e.g. JavaScript. However, they allow some events to be fired non-deterministically by user actions, I/O timing, etc. These nondeterminisms may create unexpected execution orders of event handlers, and may cause data conflicts consequently.

3 Motivation

3.1 Motivating Example 1

```
1   document.addEventListener("deviceready", onDeviceReady, false);
2   document.addEventListener("resume", refreshData, false);
3   var gpackages=[];
4   function onDeviceReady() {
5      checkConnection();
6      ......
7      if(action=="showPackages"){
8      gpackages=new Object;
9      gpackages=results;
10     ......
11  }
12  var packeti=0;
13  function refreshData(){
14     checkConnection();
15     packeti=0;
16     var len = gpackages.rows.length;
17     if(len>0 && connected==1){
18        showActivity();
19        getPackage();
20     }
21  }
```

Fig. 1. Nondeterministic scheduling of the lifecycle events.

We consider a code segment of a PhoneGap app in Fig. 1. Assuming that the code were all loaded, and the lifecycle events of the app are fired simultaneously (i.e. deviceready and resume registered by two event listener APIs at line 1, 2 respectively). As a consequence, it may dispatch nondeterministic schedules of such two lifecycle events. In other words, the corresponding event handler of deviceready can be processed before/after that of resume nondeterministically, so we can find out a data race for the shared global variable between them, gpackages at line 8 and line 16.

3.2 Motivating Example 2

Figure 2 illustrates a code segment containing two events for resource access. These events are triggered to read and update the contact of a mobile platform at line 12 and line 1 respectively. Supposing that the code were all loaded, and such two events are triggered simutanously. Afterwards, the corresponding event handler of updating the phone number (`contact.phoneNumbers[0]` at line 4) might be executed before/after it reads all phone numbers at line 15, inclusive with the first mobile number `contact.phoneNumbers[0]` nondeterministically. Consequently, it can raise a data conflict between such events for `phoneNumbers[0]` of the contact list.

```
1   navigator.contacts.find(fields, sucessUpdate, onError, options);
2   function sucessUpdate(contacts) {
3       var contact = contacts[0];
4       contact.phoneNumbers[0] = document.getElementById("phone").value;
5       contact.name = document.getElementById("name").value;
6       contact.save(function(saveSuccess) {
7           alert("Contact successful update");
8       }, function(saveError){
9           alert("Error when updating");
10      });
11  }
12  navigator.contacts.find(fields, sucessRead, onError, options);
13      function sucessRead(contacts) {
14      for(var i=0; i<contacts.length; i++) {
15          var phoneNumber = contacts[i].phoneNumbers;
16          checkphoneNumber(phoneNumber);
17      }
18  }
```

Fig. 2. Nondeterministic scheduling of the resource access events.

4 Asynchronous Middleware Framework Events

4.1 Lifecycle Events

There are several lifecycle events provided by PhoneGap for restoring and saving states of a PhoneGap app like the lifecycle of an activity in native Android apps. However, the lifecycle events of a PhoneGap app are not always guaranteed to line up with the Android's lifecycle, and they can be triggered asynchronously in a mobile web browser. A native Android app basically consists of a series of activities. The activities can be thought of as individual screens for making up the app. Different tasks in the app often have their own activity, and each activity has its own lifecycle that signals it to enter and leave the foreground of a user's mobile device. Meanwhile, a PhoneGap app executed on Webview of the Android platform is embedded into one single Android activity, and the life cycles of this activity are exposed to the PhoneGap app through firing web document objects. For example, the lifecycle event, *deviceready* fires when a PhoneGap app is fully loaded on HTML document. Once this event is fired, you can safely make calls to the

PhoneGap APIs for resource access. This event is essential to any PhoneGap app, and it is roughly equivalent to the Android's lifecycle function *onCreate()* for signaling the app starting. We consider three lifecycle events supported by PhoneGap [43] at below as they are commonly used in apps. Such events are asynchronously registered in an app by calling the listener event API, *window.addEventListener()*.

Deviceready. This event fires when a PhoneGap app is fully loaded, and it is essential to any application. It signals that PhoneGap's device APIs have already loaded on a browser and are ready to access.

Pause. This event fires when the native platform puts the application into the background, typically when an user switches to a different application.

Resume. The resume event fires when the native platform pulls the application out from the background.

4.2 Resource Access Events

Additionally, PhoneGap framework provides various sources of asynchronous events for assuring the real-time characteristic of smartphones when an app accesses to the platform resources such as contact, database, etc. More specifically, we consider the asynchronous events [41] commonly used in an app as the following categories, and such events are fired by executing directly JavaScript APIs integrated into PhoneGap.

Contact. These events are used to request the contact information such as first name, last name, phone number, etc. of a mobile platform. For example, the PhoneGap JavaScript API, *navigator.contacts.find* is used to trigger this type of events.

GPS location. These events are asynchronously triggered once the GPS location of a mobile device is requested. As an example, the PhoneGap JavScript API *navigator.geolocation.watchPosition* is used to trigger such events.

Database. These events are used to access to database system in a mobile platform. For instance, *window.sqlitePlugin.openDatabase().transaction.*

Barcode scanner. These events are fired when any barcode is scanned. For example, the JavaScript API triggers these events, *window.plugins.barcodeScanner.scan.*

File. These events force asynchronously when any file request is made. The JavaScript APIs are implemented to force them such as *window.requestFileSystem*, *directoryReader.readEntries.*

File Transfer. These events are forced once any file is transferred such as uploading a file to a server, downloading a file from a server. Their JavaScript APIs are implemented like *FileTransfer.upload, FileTransfer.download.*

5 Methodology

5.1 Event Traces

Our approach does not aim at tracing sequences of operations in an app as the previous approaches [1, 3, 5, 8, 15–18, 20]. In practice, it seems to be impossible to trace all sequences in large-scale JavaScript programs as challenges such as dynamisms, event propagation, etc., so such trace execution may miss potential sequences. Instead, our approach slices the API calls for registering/triggering the asynchronous events defined in a program. Such slice execution can cover all API calls in any JavaScript-based program without suffering the challenges. For example, the event listener API *document.addEventListener("deviceready",onDeviceReady,false)* is loaded to register the lifecycle event *deviceready*, whenever the JavaScript API *navigator.contacts.find* is directly called for firing an resource access event in order to eventually get the contact of a mobile system.

Given a collection of API calls is traced from a given app starting from the first API call ($A1$) to the last API call (An) as (1).

$$A = \{A1, A2, A3, \ldots, An\} \tag{1}$$

Next, it applies the principle of combinations in the math to create a list of pairs (P) so that two API calls for registering/firing two events per pair as (2). Pi is the last pair. For example, there are 10 API calls ($n = 10$) sliced from an app, then it generates a possible list of 45 pairs ($P = 45$) of two API calls ($k = 2$) as (3).

$$P = \{P1(A1, A2), P2(A1, A3), \ldots, Pi(A(n-1), An)\} \tag{2}$$

$$C_k^n = \frac{n!}{k!(n-k)!} = \frac{10!}{2!(10-2)!} = 45\ pairs \tag{3}$$

5.2 Happens-Before Analysis

The happens-before relation is a relation between the corresponding event handlers of two events registered/triggered by two API calls, and one event should happen before another event. Comparing with the previous work [1, 3, 5, 8, 15–18, 20], they analyzed happens-before relationship in each sequence of operations collected from a program. Meanwhile, we collect a list of the pairs by our event traces. We then implement happens-before analysis for each pair based on modeling happens-before rules as the related techniques [15–18, 20]. More specifically, we define a happens-before rule for identifying happens-before relationship in each pair based on the fact. If the corresponding event handlers of two API calls are nested, then there exist happens-before relations between them. In contrast to it, such two event handlers could be concurrently executed to generate nondeterministic schedules.

We define callback functions as the event handlers in our modeled rule because the callback functions are more frequently used in JavaScript-based web apps [14] and also in asynchronous event handling [44]. In addition, we also model various forms of the callback functions consisting of named callbacks, anonymous callbacks for improving the soundness of our data flow analysis. For example, Fig. 3 illustrates that the corresponding callback functions of two API calls for triggering the events are nested. The first API call is used to trigger the event for the file transfer (`fileTransfer.download` at line 6). The second API call is used to force the event for accessing to the file system (window.requestFileSystem at line 1). When they are carried out, the event handler of one API is executed first another one.

```
1   window.requestFileSystem(LocalFileSystem.PERSISTENT, 0, func-
2   tion(fileSystem) {
3     fileSystem.root.getFile(localFileName, {create: true, exclusive:
4   false}, function(fileEntry) {
5       try{
6       var fileTransfer = new FileTransfer();
7       fileTransfer.download(srcurl,filePath,var fileTransfer = new
8   FileTransf
```

Fig. 3. Nested callback functions between two API calls.

Algorithm 1: Detecting vulnerable pairs

> **input :** *A HTML5-based mobile app*
> **output:** *A list of vulnerable pairs*

1 *pairs ← collectOperations();*
2 *foreach pair in pairs do*
3   *edges ← computeDataflow(pair.first, pair.second);*
4   *reverseEdges ← computeDataFlow(pair.second, pair.first);*
5   *if edges is empty && reverseEdges is empty then*
6   *shared ← isSharedResources(pair.first, pair.second);*
7   *if shared then*
8   *reportVulPair(pair.first, pair.second);*

5.3 Implementation

Information Flow Propagation. We implemented our automated detection relying on TAJS [42], a powerful framework for analyzing JavaScript-based programs. Algorithm 1 shows it through two main steps as follows. Initially, given an HTML5-based mobile app and eventually reporting vulnerable pairs in the app.

Step 1. It first parses HTML files and JavaScript files of the given app into a control flow graph. Then, it executes our event traces by *collectOperations()* at line 1 for tracing the predefined API calls on the control flow graph. As a result, it creates a list of pairs so that each pair consists of two API calls for registering/firing two events. We model some asynchronous PhoneGap APIs for firing the resource access events as listed in top weakly downloads [41], and the event listener APIs for registering the PhoneGap lifecycle events as shown in Tables 1 and 2 respectively.

Step 2. For each pair, it computes data flow between two API calls by applying the interprocedural forward analysis for analyzing happens-before relations based on the modeled rule. It scans the forward edges starting from the first API call to the second API call and the reverse edges starting from the second API call to the first one by *computeDataFlow()* at line 3, 4. When both two sets are empty, it means having no nested API calls or the event handlers of two API calls are not nested, as a result, they may be handled concurrently.

More specifically, in *computeDataFlow()*, it slices the callback functions of one API call. Traverse through each callback function, it checks whether another API in the pair is included in the callback function. If so, the corresponding callback handlers between the API calls are nested or they are synchronized, so it will continue to process the next pair. If not so, the callback handlers of two API calls could be executed concurrently. In this case, it will track if the callback handlers of them can happen data races through *isSharedResources()* at line 6.

In detail, in *isSharedResources()*, it slices the shared global objects that are defined as the global scope between the handler functions of them. Afterwards, it monitors whether the callback handlers of either one or two API calls perform write operations to the shared objects. If so, it will flag the pair as a vulnerable pair by *reportVulPair()* at line 8.

Limitation. In fact, it remains many challenges in information flow analysis for JavaScript-based programs. First of all, the impact of code changes through event propagation, etc. can generate invisible data flow in apps [21–23]. Our data flow analysis is unable to monitor such invisible connections. Last but not least, our analysis is also limited by dynamic information flow due to the highly dynamic features of JavaScript code.

Table 1. The PhoneGap APIs are called for firing the resource access events.

Category	API
File	window.requestFileSystem directoryReader.readEntries
File transfer	FileTransfer.upload FileTransfer.download
SQLite storage	window.sqlitePlugin.openDatabase().transaction
Geolocation	navigator.geolocation.watchPosition
Contact	navigator.contacts.find intel.xdk.contacts.getContactData intel.xdk.contacts.editContact intel.xdk.contacts.get
Barcode scanner	window.plugins.barcodeScanner.scan

Manual Code Inspection. We apply a manual code inspection of the vulnerable pairs for detecting true data races between events because the vulnerable pairs may provoke

Table 2. The event listener APIs are loaded to register the PhoneGap lifecycle events.

Event	API
Deviceready	window.addEventListener('deviceready', function(…))
Resume	window.addEventListener('resume', function(…))
Pause	window.addEventListener('pause', function(….))

harmless races. Here, we define that a harmful race occurs if there exists any execution order of the event handlers that causes data inconsistency for a shared object in the global scope. The global object shared between event handlers is considered as global variables and the platform resources such as contact, database, etc. Meanwhile, a harmless race or a false positive occurs whether there exists happens-before relationship between two API calls, so the event handlers cannot be concurrently processed. For example, harmless races can be found since our data flow analysis is not capable to analyze some complex structures of JavaScript programs, so it can report false alarms. Last but not least, harmless races can be occurred as our analysis is unable to analyze indirect data flow such as event propagation, JavaScript dynamism, etc. as presented in [21–23].

6 Evaluation

In this evaluation, our purpose measures the effectiveness of our approach in term of how many event-based races it detects. To perform it, we downloaded 1,926 HTML5-based mobile apps from Google Play Stores and third-party stores. The list includes the PhoneGap apps provided by Lau et al. [27], and the apps have developed from the year 2012 to 2018. Since many apps in the previous list were removed from stores, we were able to gather a dataset of 1,926 apps. We implemented the automated detection in about 300 Java LOC extended from TAJS [42] in addition to circumscribing the average detection time per app by around 50 s. The hardware configuration for this evaluation is set up 2.2-GHz Intel Core i7 CPU, 16 GB RAM.

6.1 Effectiveness

Our approach effectiveness. First of all, we ran our automated detection to analyze a dataset of 1,926 apps. As a result, it flagged out 18 vulnerable apps consisting of 23 vulnerable pairs, and the average detection time for one app costs around 30 s. Afterwards, we manually conducted an additional step to inpsect 23 vulnerable pairs by manually creating possible schedules of events from each vulnerable pair. The process of this manual code review took about an hour. We discovered 8 out of 23 pairs as 8 false positives, and 21 harmful races out of 15 remaining vulnerable pairs. Such eight false alarms are occured due to the imprecision of the data flow analysis, so it is unable to track happens-before relationship in these pairs. Note that, each vulnerable pair can raise more data races between events.

Comparing with other approaches. We have to admit that our evaluation is limited by quantitatively comparing the effectiveness of our approach to other approaches [1, 3, 5, 8, 15–18, 20] due to some following possible reasons. First of all, our target apps are different from the other approaches aiming at native Android apps and web apps. For example, the approaches [1, 3, 5, 8] require to instrument a web browser, so we have to implement those approaches so as to instrument a mobile browser (e.g. WebView in Android, WKWebView in iOS). In addition, even though the previous work [15–18, 20] applied static analysis for race detection in native Android apps, this type of apps are written in Java code, so it is very hard to implement them applicable to JavaScript-based programs.

Soundness. Analyzing JavaScript-based programs still remains many challenges because of their dynamisms, so there may exist potential pairs our approach missed or was incapable to identify whether they are false positives or true positives. Moreover, some races may occur by dynamic data flow appearing at runtime. Therefore, it may remains more false negatives in the dataset as these challenges.

6.2 Event-Based Races

We found out totally 21 real event-based races, including 5 data races caused by the lifecycle events and 16 races come from firing the resource access events. Such races fit into the following categories as shown in Fig. 4.

Database events. This type of events are fired to access to local database storages in a mobile platform. Finally, there are totally 9 data races occuring by firing them.

File request events. These events are used to request location of file system which is not a part of the sandboxed storage system. Especially, we picked out 3 data races between such events.

Contact events. These events are created to access to the contact of a mobile system. We discovered 4 out of 16 event-based races.

Lifecycle events. These events are used to restore and save states of an app. Eventually, we detected 5 data races among these events (*deviceready*, *resume*).

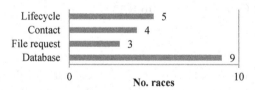

Fig. 4. The categories of the event-based races are detected in the dataset.

7   Related Work

Event-based races in web apps. The previous researches proposed various techniques by instrumenting into the web browser to dynamically trace sequences of operations in apps [1, 3, 5, 8]. WAVE [1] and R4 [5] applied test execution on the traced sequences as test cases for detecting races. AJAXRACER [3] implemented an event-based graph for identifying AJAX event races on the graph. Moreover, Adamsen et al. [2] presented an approach to repair event-based races in apps automatically. Zhang et al. [9] aimed at classifying harmful and harmless races. Our work focuses on scanning races occured by firing middleware framework events in HTML5-based mobile apps. Comparing with these techniques, our approach applies the static detection for identifying happens-before relations in pairs of two API calls for firing events.

Event-based races in mobile apps. Several research papers resolved event-driven races in native mobile apps, especially, in native Android apps [15–18, 20]. The event-based races are common sources of concurrency bugs rather than data races in multi-threads in Android apps [16]. Hsiao et al. [18] applied a conventional causality model integrated into the stack of the Android framework for identifying races in apps. Hu et al. [16] proposed SIERRA using static analysis to scan race in inter-components in apps. Bielik et al. [17] presented an approach to statically find races in the UI thread. ERVA [15] is developed for distinguishing benign races from harmful races. Tang et al. [20] leveraged test execution to generate test cases exposing concurrency bugs in Android apps. Our work targets to HTML5-based mobile apps developed by leveraging standard web technologies.

Event-based errors. Some previous researchers presented various methods to find specific types of errors as a result of happening event-based races. Madsen et al. [6] described four types of the errors consisting of dead listener, dead emits, mismatched synchronous and asynchronous calls in Node.js-based apps. Wang et al. [7] conducted a comprehensive study of concurrency errors in Node.js apps. Fan et al. [19] introduced APEChecker to detect programming errors in asynchronous interactions, including hard-to-detect, fail-stop in Android apps. Alimadadi et al. [11] presented the issues in asynchronous interactions for full-stack JavaScript. Alimadadi et al. [12] described broken promises in JavaScript-based programs. Moreover, Patra et al. [13] proposed ConflictJS, an automated and a scalable approach to detect data conflicts for JavaScript libraries. Our work aims at finding event-based races.

Data races in multi-threaded programs. Data races in standard multi-threaded programs such as Java, C/C++ have received much attention from research community. Several well-known approaches were introduced to detect such data races [23–25]. For instance, FastTrack [23] is a dynamic analysis tool for detecting data races in multi-threaded Java programs. Grace [24] is a powerful tool for identifying the races in multi-threaded C/C++ programs. Analyzing event-based raced in JavaScript-based programms is much more challenging than standard multi-threaded programs because JavaScript code is a highly dynamic programming language.

HTML5-based mobile apps. There is a little work paying attention to the issues of such hybrid mobile apps [27–36]. Jin et al. [29] found a new vector of code injection attacks through exploiting sensitive plugin APIs integrated into PhoneGap. Lau et al. [27] implemented data flow analysis to scan code injection flaws in apps. Yang et al. [30] presented event-oriented exploits that can trigger critical functionalities in Android hybrid apps for causing resource access, data leaks, etc. Rizzo et al. [32] and Hu et al. [36] presented WebView issues, including code injection attacks on WebView and how

WebView induces bugs to Android apps. Georgiev et al. [31] found a new class of attacks (so called fracking attacks) that can leak the sensitive system resources to untrusted websites. Additionally, Phung et al. [34] and Wang et al. [35] proposed access control mechanisms to restrict invocations to the platform resources. Lau et al. [37] introduced an attack vector that can pose serious threats, including data leaks and resource access by remotely triggering JavaScript framework events defined in apps. In this paper, we present event-based races that can cause data conflicts for the platform resources in HTML5-based mobile apps.

8   Conclusion

Because HTML5-based mobile apps leverage standard web technologies, they may be subject to face with event-based races resulting from triggering user events, system events, network events as web apps. The races in such hybrid mobile apps can come from various sources of asynchronous events, in particular, middleware framework events. A middleware framework acted as a communication bridge provides the resource access events for communicating with the native system functionalities such as database, contact, SMS, etc. and the lifecycle events like Android's lifecycle for signaling states of an app.

In this paper, we present event-based races in HTML5-based mobile apps. Additionally, we also introduce a semi-automated approach based on combining the data flow analysis with the manual code analysis for identifying real races. In our evaluation, we executed it on a dataset of 1,926 HTML5-based mobile apps. As a result, it flagged out 18 vulnerable apps. Furthermore, we manually inspected such vulnerable apps and figured out 21 true races.

References

1. Hong, S, Park, Y., Kim, M.: Detecting concurrency errors in client-side JavaScript web applications. In: Proceedings of Software Testing, Verification and Validation (ICST), pp. 61–70 (2014)
2. Adamsen, C.Q., Møller, A., Karim, R., Sridharan, M., Tip, F., Sen, K.: Repairing event race errors by controlling nondeterminism. In: Proceedings of the 39th International Conference on Software Engineering (ICSE), pp. 289–299 (2017)
3. Adamsen, C.Q., Møller, A., Alimadadi, S., Tip, F.: Practical AJAX race detection for JavaScript web applications. In: Proceedings of the 26th ACM Joint Meeting on European Software Engineering Conference and Symposium on the Foundations of Software Engineering (ESEC/FSE), pp. 38–48 (2018)
4. Adamsen, C.Q., Møller, A., Tip, F.: Practical initialization race detection for JavaScript web applications (OOPLAS). In: Proceedings of the ACM on Programming Languages, p. 66 (2017)
5. Adamsen, C.Q., Møller, A., Raychev, V., Dimitrov, D., Vechev, M.: Stateless model checking of event-driven applications. In: ACM SIGPLAN Notices, vol. 50, no. 10, pp. 57–73 (2015)
6. Madsen, M., Tip, F., Lhoták, O.: Static analysis of event-driven Node.js JavaScript applications. In: ACM SIGPLAN Notices, vol. 50, no. 10, pp. 505–519 (2015)

7. Wang, J., et al.: A comprehensive study on real world concurrency bugs in Node.js. In: Proceedings of the 32nd IEEE/ACM International Conference on Automated Software Engineering (ASE), pp. 520–531 (2017)
8. Raychev, V., Vechev, M., Sridharan, M.: Effective race detection for event-driven programs. In: ACM SIGPLAN Notices, vol. 48, no. 10, pp. 151–166 (2013)
9. Zhang, L, Wang, C.: RClassify: classifying race conditions in web applications via deterministic replay. In: Proceedings of the 39th International Conference on Software Engineering (ICSE), pp. 278–288 (2017)
10. Alimadadi, S., Sequeira, S., Mesbah, A., Pattabiraman, K.: Understanding JavaScript event-based interactions. In: Proceedings of the 36th International Conference on Software Engineering (ICSE), pp. 367–377 (2014)
11. Alimadadi, S, Mesbah, A., Pattabiraman, K.: Understanding asynchronous interactions in full-stack JavaScript. In: Proceedings of the 38th International Conference on Software Engineering (ICSE), pp. 1169–1180 (2016)
12. Alimadadi, S., Zhong, D., Madsen, M., Tip, F.: Finding broken promises in asynchronous JavaScript programs. In: Proceedings of the ACM on Programming Languages (OOPSLA) (2018)
13. Patra, J., Dixit, P.N., Pradel, M.: ConflictJS: finding and understanding conflicts between JavaScript libraries. In: Proceedings of the 40th International Conference on Software Engineering (ICSE), pp. 741–751 (2018)
14. Gallaba, L., Mesbah, A., Beschastnikh, I.: Don't call us, we'll call you: characterizing callbacks in JavaScript. In: Proceedings of Empirical Software Engineering and Measurement (ESEM), pp. 1–10 (2015)
15. Hu, Y., Neamtiu, I., Alavi, A.: Automatically verifying and reproducing event-based races in Android apps. In: Proceedings of the 25th International Symposium on Software Testing and Analysis (ISSTA), pp. 377–388 (2016)
16. Hu, Y., Neamtiu, I.: Static detection of event-based races in Android apps. In: Proceedings of the Twenty-Third International Conference on Architectural Support for Programming Languages and Operating Systems (ASPLOS), pp. 257–270 (2018)
17. Bielik, P., Raychev, V., Vechev, M.: Scalable race detection for Android applications. In: ACM SIGPLAN Notices, vol. 50, no. 10, pp. 332–348 (2015)
18. Hsiao, C.H., et al.: Race detection for event-driven mobile applications. In: ACM SIGPLAN Notices, vol. 49, no. 6, pp. 326–336 (2014)
19. Fan, L., et al.: Efficiently manifesting asynchronous programming errors in Android apps. In: Proceedings of the 33rd ACM/IEEE International Conference on Automated Software Engineering (ASE), pp. 486–497 (2018)
20. Tang, H., Wu, G., Wei, J., Zhong, H.: Generating test cases to expose concurrency bugs in android applications. In: Proceedings of the 31st IEEE/ACM International Conference on Automated Software Engineering (ASE), pp. 648–653 (2016)
21. Murthy, D.R., Pradel, M.: Change-aware dynamic program analysis for JavaScript. In: Proceedings of the IEEE International Conference on Software Maintenance and Evolution (ICSME), pp. 127–137 (2018)
22. Alimadadi, S., Mesbah, A., Pattabiraman, K.: Hybrid DOM-sensitive change impact analysis for JavaScript. In: LIPIcs-Leibniz International Proceedings in Informatics (2015)
23. Sung, C., Kusano, M., Sinha, N., Wang, C.: Static DOM event dependency analysis for testing web applications. In: Proceedings of the 24th ACM SIGSOFT International Symposium on Foundations of Software Engineering, pp. 447–459 (2016)
24. Flanagan, C., Freund, S.N.: FastTrack: efficient and precise dynamic race detection. In: ACM SIGPLAN Notices, vol. 44, no. 6, pp. 121–133 (2009)
25. Berger, E.D., Yang, T., Liu, T., Novark, G.: Grace: safe multithreaded programming for C/C++. In: ACM SIGPLAN Notices, vol. 44, no. 10, pp. 81–96 (2009)

26. Lu, K., Zhou, X., Bergan, T., Wang, X.: Efficient deterministic multithreading without global barriers. In: ACM SIGPLAN Notices, vol. 49, no. 8, pp. 287–300 (2014)
27. Lau, P.T.: Scan code injection flaws in HTML5-based mobile applications. In: Proceedings of the IEEE International Conference on Software Testing, Verification and Validation Workshops (ICSTW), pp. 81–88 (2018)
28. Yang, G., Huang, J., Gu, G., Mendoza, A.: Study and mitigation of origin stripping vulnerabilities in hybrid-postmessage enabled mobile applications. In: IEEE Symposium on Security and Privacy (SP), pp. 742–755 (2018)
29. Jin, X., et al.: Code injection attacks on HTML5-based mobile apps: characterization, detection, mitigation. In: Proceedings of the ACM SIGSAC Conference on Computer and Communications Security (CCS), pp. 66–77 (2014)
30. Yang, G., Huang, J., Gu, G.: Automated generation of event-oriented exploits in android hybrid apps. In: Network and Distributed System Security Symposium (NDSS) (2018)
31. Yang, G., Huang, J., Gu, G., Mendoza, A.: Study and mitigation of origin stripping vulnerabilities in hybrid-postmessage enabled mobile applications. In: Proceedings of Symposium on Security and Privacy (SP), pp. 742–755 (2018)
32. Georgiev, M., Jana, S., Shmatikov, V.: Breaking and fixing origin based access control in hybrid web/mobile application frameworks. In: Network and Distributed System Security Symposium (NDSS) (2014)
33. Rizzo, C., Cavallaro, L., Kinder, J.: BabelView: evaluating the impact of code injection attacks in mobile webviews. In: International Symposium on Research in Attacks, Intrusions, and Defenses, pp. 25–46 (2018)
34. Phung, P.H., Mohanty, A., Rachapalli, R., Sridhar, M.: Hybridguard: a principal-based permission and fine-grained policy enforcement framework for web-based mobile applications. In: Security and Privacy Workshops (SPW), pp. 147–156 (2017)
35. Jin, X., Wang, L., Luo, T., Du, W.: Fine-grained access control for HTML5-based mobile applications in android. In: Information Security, pp. 309–318 (2015)
36. Hu, J., Wei, L., Liu, Y., Heung, S.C., Huang, H.: A tale of two cities: how WebView induces bugs to Android applications. In: Proceedings of the 33rd ACM/IEEE International Conference on Automated Software Engineering (ASE), pp. 702–713 (2018)
37. Lau, P.T.: Event-based remote attacks in HTML5-based mobile apps. In: Proceedings of the 2nd International Workshop on Information and Operational Technology Security Systems (IOSec) (2019, in press)
38. PhoneGap: Build amazing mobile apps powered by open web tech. https://phonegap.com
39. Ionic. https://ionicframework.com/docs/v1/concepts/structure.html
40. Framework 7. https://facebook.github.io/react-native/
41. PhoneGap plugin APIs. https://cordova.apache.org/plugins/
42. https://github.com/cs-au-dk/TAJS
43. PhoneGap lifecycle events. https://cordova.apache.org/docs/en/latest/cordova/events/events.html
44. Asynchronous JavaScript programs. http://callbackhell.com/

Analysing Security Protocols Using Scenario Based Simulation

Farah Al-Shareefi[✉], Alexei Lisitsa, and Clare Dixon

Department of Computer Science, University of Liverpool, Liverpool L69 3BX, UK
{F.M.A.Al-Shareefi,lisitsa,cldixon}@liverpool.ac.uk

Abstract. In this paper, we present a methodology for analysing security protocols using scenario based simulation. A scenario of a potential attack specifies the flow but not the content of messages. Using scenarios can reduce the number of protocol runs to be explored during attack searching via simulation. The number of runs can be further reduced by minimizing the number of intruder's generated messages. The intruder's ability to generate messages is limited by considering: the expected message content and type matching. Our approach uses two tools that support the Abstract State Machines method: the AsmetaL for modelling purposes and the AsmetaS for performing the simulation. We propose a simple model for the specification of commutative encryption. Several protocols are examined to show the effectiveness of our method.

Keywords: Security protocols · Abstract State Machines · Protocol simulation · Attack scenarios

1 Introduction

Various formal analysis approaches have been developed for designing correct and secure protocols. Many of these approaches, which depend on the intruder Dolev-Yao model [10], assume the following: (1) the intruder can generate any message it wants based on its knowledge; (2) the encryption mechanism is unbreakable without knowing the related decryption key; and (3) the intruder can launch an unbounded number of sessions.

The first assumption may lead to some superfluous messages with wrong format or type, are likely to be rejected by the honest participants. The second assumption may be too strong in some contexts. In particular, some encryption mechanisms with certain algebraic properties can be broken [18], for instance commutative encryption [21]. The third assumption together with the first one generally leads to undecidability of the verification problem due to unbounded state space to be analysed. Some tools, e.g., ProVerif and Tamarin [4,22], have addressed state space explosion problem but at the cost of possible non-termination of the analysis, particularly in the presence of non-trivial algebraic properties, such as the one of commutative encryption. The work in [16] deals with the undecidable verification problem by simulating security protocols using

© Springer Nature Switzerland AG 2019
P. Ganty and M. Kaâniche (Eds.): VECoS 2019, LNCS 11847, pp. 47–62, 2019.
https://doi.org/10.1007/978-3-030-35092-5_4

scenarios designed for the message origin and destination attacks [25]. A scenario is a protocol run composed of multiple sessions in which the pattern of ordering the protocol steps for the involved sessions is specified. This approach is an effective way for reducing the number of protocol runs, while looking for an attack by simulation. However, the intruder in this work composes messages using only type matching restriction, which may still increase the message space with unacceptable messages.

Building upon this development, we propose our methodology to analyse security protocols taking into account reducing the search space by simulating only the protocol runs that are specified by the attack scenarios, modelling a "clever" intruder who generates only acceptable messages, and considering the commutative property. Typically, we restrict message generation by focusing on two issues: the supposed message type format and the expected message content. We model commutative encryption in a simple procedural way that can capture its commutativity property, i.e. $\{\{m\}_{k_a}\}_{k_b} = \{\{m\}_{k_b}\}_{k_a}$. Furthermore, we adopt and update the attack scenarios in the analysis step. Our method is supported by the Abstract State Machine (ASM) method [6]. We, note that ASM method does not directly support the commutativity property and it needs to be encoded. This method has an executable language, called the ASMETA Language (AsmetaL) [14], which is used to specify the protocol, the intruder, and the attack scenarios, and a simulator tool, known as ASMETA Simulator (AsmetaS) [13], which is employed to simulate the protocol runs controlled by the specified scenario. As examples, we analyse the Needham-Schroder (NS) public key protocol [23], and the Three-Pass (TP) protocol [24].

The main contributions of this paper are: (1) formulating a principle for generating messages by the intruder according to the receiver's expectations. This takes into consideration the message type format and the expected content; (2) using the attack pattern scenarios in the actual verification/validation process based on simulation in the ASM methodology; (3) modelling commutative encryption and analysing protocols in the presence of this algebraic property.

The paper is structured as follows: Sect. 2 details the ASM method and security protocols. Section 3 introduces our methodology in general and discusses its aspects in details, including modelling of the protocol, the intruder, the attack scenarios, as well as specifying the invariant conditions. Results and discussion are discussed in Sect. 4, whereas Sect. 5 reviews related work. Section 6 concludes the paper.

2   Background

2.1   Abstract State Machines

Abstract State Machines (ASMs) are a versatile formal method for engineering any computational system in a mathematically well-grounded way [5,6]. ASMs are transition systems with configurations representing *abstract states* and transition relations defined by *rules*. The abstract states are multi-sorted first order structure states, i.e, universes of elements coming with many type functions and predicates declared on them. ASM transition rules specify how function interpretations are updated to change the current state into the next one. The essential form of transition rule is a *function update* $f(t_1, ..., t_n) := t$. f is an arbitrary n-ary function and $t_1, ..., t_n$ are first-order terms, which are simultaneously evaluated to produce a new state. There are some rule constructors, such as: **if then** (conditional rule), **seq** (sequential rules execution), **par** (parallel rules execution), **extend** (expanded universe rule), and **switch case** (selected conditional rule). The functions can be classified, based on the updating way for their values, into three categories: *static* (their values are never changed in any state), *controlled* (their values are changed by the machine), and *monitored* (their values are changed by the environment).

Different toolsets and frameworks have been developed to support the ASM method, such as CoreASM[1] project [12], ASMETA[2] [14] framework, etc. In this paper, we have used the ASMETA framework, which has several tools, including the ASMETA Language (AsmetaL) and the ASMETA Simulator (AsmetaS) for editing and simulating ASM models [13]. AsmetaS supports expressing invariant constraints over functions and rules to provide a proof of AsmetaL specification's incorrectness in the violation case. The invariant is declared as follows:

$$\text{invariant } constraint\_name \text{ over } fun\_name, .., rule\_name : term$$

where invariant is a keyword related to a selected name *constraint_name* of the constraint, *fun_name* and *rule_name* are some functions and rules of specification which over them the constraint must be expressed, and *term* denotes the boolean term that expresses the constraint.

2.2 Security Protocol Notation and Examples

In this section, we use the basic notation, called Common Syntax(CS) [9], to describe the security protocols [15]. A protocol is a finite sequence of steps for exchanging messages between participants having their roles, including initiator, responder, and server. Each step has the following form: $i. X_i \rightarrow Y_i : M_i$, where $1 \leqslant i \leqslant n$, is the ith protocol step, $X_i(Y_i)$ is the sender(receiver) of step i, respectively, and M_i is the message of step i. The X_i and Y_i could be honest participants with A, B identities, or a trusted third-party server with S identity. A message may contain one or more *encrypted* or *unencrypted* components (or fields), which follow either public key encryption method or symmetric key encryption method. The unencrypted component is either an identity, key, fresh component, such as nonces or timestamps, or just text. The encrypted component, usually denoted as $\{m\}_k$, is a protocol message or sub message encrypted using the key k. The key is expressed using the following notations: $ssk(X, Y)$ denoting a symmetric shared key between X and Y participants, $pk(X)$ and $prk(X)$ representing the participant's public and private keys. Usually, the participant identities and the message content are represented as variables in the protocol specification. A *single session* of a protocol is an instantiation of these variables to generate a sequence of concrete identities and message content.

---

[1] http://www.coreasm.org/.

[2] http://asmeta.sourceforge.net/.

Multiple sessions are several instantiated sequences (possibly interleaved) with their own identifier numbers for distinguishing them. A *protocol run* is a concrete instantiation for a sequence of protocol steps resulting from a fixed number of multiple sessions, that are possibly parallel.

An attack on a protocol is a protocol run that satisfies an undesirable property, such as revealing a secret. Launching an attack on a protocol is performed by a deceptive participant called intruder with I identity. The $I(X)$ notation mean that the intruder impersonates the honest participant with X acting.

An attack scenario is an abstracted protocol run, which is specified according to known attacks, where the message content is abstracted away. In fact, a scenario does not specify the message content, except the repetition case of previously sent messages which can be identified. A scenario has predefined information about assigning the participant identities and the intruder impersonations to each participant's role, see Fig. 1. Figure 1 presents an example of Man In The Middle (MITM) attack scenario. The left column of

$$1.1\ A \rightarrow I \quad : \ M_1$$
$$2.1\ I(A) \rightarrow B : \ M_1$$
$$2.2\ B \rightarrow I(A) : \ M_2$$
$$1.2\ I \rightarrow A \quad : \ M_2$$
$$1.3\ A \rightarrow I \quad : \ M_3$$
$$2.3\ I(A) \rightarrow B : \ M_3$$

Fig. 1. An example of MITM attack scenario

this figure shows a pattern of ordering the protocol steps for the involved sessions in which an assignment of the identities and intruder impersonation to each participant's role has been defined. While the right column manifests a metavariable M_i, which has a value specified by the intruder or the honest participants.

We illustrate our method using two protocols: the Needham-Schroder (NS) public key protocol [23], and the Three-Pass (TP) protocol [21,24]. NS protocol aims to achieve mutual authentication between two participants A and B, see Fig. 2a. In this protocol, A and B are convinced that they are communicating with the intended correspondent, since they believe that they only know about the newly generated nonces N_A and N_B. However, this is incorrect, as the protocol subjects to the MITM attack [20] shown in Fig. 2b. Note that, the attack in Fig. 2b is an instance of the scenario in Fig. 1.

$$1.\ A \rightarrow B : \{A, N_A\}_{pk(B)}$$
$$2.\ B \rightarrow A : \{N_A, N_B\}_{pk(A)}$$
$$3.\ A \rightarrow B : \{N_B\}_{pk(B)}$$

(a) The NS protocol's messages

$$1.1\ A \rightarrow I \quad : \{A, N_A\}_{pk(I)}$$
$$2.1\ I(A) \rightarrow B : \{A, N_A\}_{pk(B)}$$
$$2.2\ B \rightarrow I(A) : \{N_A, N_B\}_{pk(A)}$$
$$1.2\ I \rightarrow A \quad : \{N_A, N_B\}_{pk(A)}$$
$$1.3\ A \rightarrow I \quad : \{N_B\}_{pk(I)}$$
$$2.3\ I(A) \rightarrow B : \{N_B\}_{pk(B)}$$

(b) The Lowe attack on NS protocol

Fig. 2. The NS protocol example

The TP protocol [21,24] is designed to securely transmit a message over an insecure network, without sharing or distributing any secret. The encryption mechanism for TP protocol is assumed to satisfy the commutative property, i.e.,

$\{\{m\}_{prk(A)}\}_{prk(B)} = \{\{m\}_{prk(B)}\}_{prk(A)}$, where the encryption and decryption functions are the same. The protocol is shown in Fig. 3a. Upon receiving the second message, A decrypts it with its private key $prk(A)$, and sends the encryption output to B at the third step. There are several attacks on this protocol [8], that exploit the commutative property to compromise the secret message, as shown in Fig. 3b and c.

1. $A \rightarrow B : \{m\}_{prk(A)}$
2. $B \rightarrow A : \{\{m\}_{prk(A)}\}_{prk(B)}$
3. $A \rightarrow B : \{m\}_{prk(B)}$

(a) The TP protocol's messages

1.1 $A \rightarrow I(B)$: $\{m\}_{prk(A)}$
1.2 $I(B) \rightarrow A$: $\{\{m\}_{prk(A)}\}_{prk(I)}$
1.3 $A \rightarrow I(B)$: $\{m\}_{prk(I)}$

(b) The first attack on TP protocol

1.1 $A \rightarrow I(B)$: $\{m\}_{prk(A)}$
2.1 $I(B) \rightarrow A$: $\{m\}_{prk(A)}$
2.2 $A \rightarrow I(B)$: m
1.2 $I(B) \rightarrow A$: $text$
1.3 $A \rightarrow I(B)$: $\{text\}_{prk(A)}$
2.3 $I(B) \rightarrow A$: $\{text\}_{prk(A)}$

(c) The second attack on TP protocol

Fig. 3. The TP protocol example

3   A Methodology for Analysing Security Protocols

Our general methodology consists of four aspects: the *protocol* aspect (a modular model for any protocol allowing to add different participants required for it), the *intruder* aspect (a general model for the intruder behaviour), the *attack scenarios* aspect (a built-in specification of attack scenarios, inspired by [16], into the intruder model to sketch its behaviour), and the *invariant security properties* aspect (invariant constraints employed for ensuring that the resulting model always meets these constraints). For any protocol, the intruder and the attack scenario aspects can be used directly without any amendment, while the rest can be used only after a simple modification based on the protocol's requirements.

Our methodology assumes that (1) there is a specific format for each message, and the honest participants only accept the messages conforming with this format. (2) The intruder is presumed to be as powerful as possible, where it can (a) intercept and eavesdrop any sent message; (b) generate new messages according to its knowledge and the allowed messages' format and content; (c) decrypt an encrypted message when it knows the decryption key or when the execution of a protocol depends on an algebraic property of the encryption method.

3.1   The Protocol Aspect

This aspect represents modelling the protocol participants and their main operations needed for message construction as AsmetaL rules. In this section, we model the NS protocol in AmetaL. We define the domain $Protocol = \{NS, TP\}$ to enumerate the protocol names. As each participant has a specific role, we construct a rule that corresponds to each role, such as *r_Initiator* rule for the initiator, see Code 1. The first step to build these rules is defining the domain $Id = \{AA,\ BB,\ II\}$ that represents the set of identities for the participants shared in the NS protocol, including the intruder.

The second step is stating the protocol's control flow, e.g., identifying when to send a message. Each participant can be in two states: *SEND* and *RECEIVE* for sending and receiving a message, respectively. The protocol's session starts when the initiator wants to initiate, i.e. when the Boolean function *wantToInit(Id)* is *true*. Each message has a number stored in the *msgNo* controlled function (a controlled function is equivalent to a variable in standard programming languages and a static function is equivalent to a constant). Similarly, the running session number is stored in the *sNo* function. To indicate a message related to a particular session is about to be sent, the *start* function is set to be *true*. To indicate a message has been received, the function *finish* is set to *true*.

```
rule r_Initiator($InId in Id, $ResId in Id)=
 if state=SEND then
  par
     if wantToInit($InId) and msgNo=1 then
       seq
           start(NS, sNo, 1):=true
           r_GenerateNc[]
           ncInt($InId, $ResId):=n
           r_Encrypt[[toString($InId), n], pk($ResId)]
           r_Send[[toString(cypher)], $InId, $ResId]
           wantToInit($InId):=false
       endseq
     endif
     if msgNo=3 and start(NS, sNo, 3)=false then
       seq
           start(NS, sNo, 3):=true
           r_Encrypt[[at(plainText, 1n)], pk($ResId)]
           r_Send[[toString(cypher)], $InId, $ResId]
       endseq
     endif
  endpar
 else
     if inBox($InId)!=undef and msgNo=2 and finish(NS, sNo, 2)=false then
       seq
           r_Decrypt[first(inBox($InId)), prk(pk($InId))]
           inBox($InId):=undef
           if plainText!=undef and
               ncInt($InId, $ResId)=first(plainText) then
                  finish(NS, sNo, 2):=true
           endif
       endseq
     endif
 endif
```

Code 1: The r_Initiator of the NS protocol

The next step shows how to define and deal with each message. The message is defined as a sequence of Strings. The participant realizes that there is a received message when its inbox has a message. Whereas a constructed message is sent by updating the *outBox* function with this message. To build a message, the participant can generate a nonce by the *r_GenerateNc* rule or encrypt a message by the *r_Encrypt* rule or decrypt it by the *r_Decrypt* rule.

We model the encryption and nonce generation operations in an abstract way, by employing the *extend* construct that expands an abstract domain for the operation outputs with a new element.

We can also specify the algebraic property of the encryption function, such as commutativity. An encryption function is called commutative if it satisfies the following condition: $\{\{m\}_{k_1}\}_{k_2} = \{\{m\}_{k_2}\}_{k_1}$, where k_1 and k_2 are encryption keys. The common ciphers that use commutative function, such as one-time-pad and Pohlig-Hellman ciphers, can be found in [21,24]. Notice that ASM specifications are abstract *imperative* programs and do not allow to simply state commutative property in declarative way. It rather has to be supported by the imperative executable semantics of ASM rules. Our specification for the commutative encryption is presented in Code 2. In this Code, we first introduce the specification signature. The *Cipher* is an infinite domain for the ciphertext. The *key* for a cipher element is defined as a set of keys. The task for this set is keeping track for all the keys that are used to encrypt a given message. The encryption function is implemented with respect to its commutative property by including or excluding the encryption key from the keys set which must initially be empty. The unary function *plain* is a sequence of Strings that stands for the plaintext of a given *Cipher* element. The *cipher* function is a sequence of String representing the encryption output.

```
dynamic abstract domain Cipher
dynamic abstract domain Key
controlled key : Cipher-> Powerset(Key)
controlled plain : Cipher-> Seq(String)
controlled cipher : Seq(String)
rule r_GenNew($n in Seq(String),$k in Powerset(Key))=
  extend Cipher with $e do
    par
        cipher:=[toString($e)]
        plain($e):=$n
        key($e):=$k
    endpar
rule r_comEncrypt($m in Seq(String), $k in Key)=
  choose $c in Cipher with length($m)=1 and toString($c)=first($m) do
  if contains(key($c), $k) and isEmpty(excluding(key($c), $k)) then
        cipher:=plain($c)
  else
    if contains(key($c), $k) then
    choose $c1 in Cipher with plain($c1)=plain($c) and
                    key($c1)=excluding(key($c), $k) do
            cipher:=[toString($c1)]
    ifnone
        r_GenNew[plain($c), excluding(key($c), $k)]
    else
    choose $c2 in Cipher with plain($c2)=plain($c) and
                    key($c2)=including(key($c), $k) do
        cipher:=[toString($c2)]
    ifnone
        r_GenNew[plain($c), including(key($c), $k)]
    endif
  endif
ifnone
    choose $c3 in Cipher with plain($c3)=$m and key($c3)=including({}, $k) do
    cipher:=[toString($c3)]
  ifnone
    r_GenNew[$m, including({}, $k)]
```

Code 2: The commutative encryption rule

After the signature we specify two rules: the *r_GenNew* and the *r_ComEncrypt*. The *r_GenNew* rule generates a ciphertext for a given message by extending the *Cipher* domain with one element. The *r_ComEncrypt* rule is responsible of returning the encryption output that satisfies the commutative property, by examining the following conditions:

(1) If the message that we want to encrypt is *plaintext* then either a new encryption output is returned by *r_GenNew*, if this message has not been encrypted before, or the previous calculated encryption output is returned.

(2) If the message that we want to encrypt is *ciphertext* then there are two situations: (a) The encryption key *does not belong to* the keys' set for this ciphertext. In this case, the encryption key will be included in the keys' set, and the *Cipher* domain is checked if it contains an element with a keys' set equal to the obtained one; otherwise the *r_GenNew* rule is called. (b) The encryption key *belongs to* the keys' set. Then, the encryption key will be excluded from this set. Later, the resultant set will be checked if it is an empty set, then the plaintext for the given ciphertext is returned as an encrypted output, else the *Cipher* domain is checked to regain an element with the same obtained keys' set, otherwise the *r_GenNew* rule is called.

3.2   The Intruder Aspect

In the classic Dolev-Yao intruder model [10], the intruder can generate and send any message based on its knowledge. This can lead to an issue of the growing message space with redundant messages which are likely to be rejected by the receiver. We solve this issue by limiting the intruder's capability to generate and send only the messages that have accepted contents and type format based on the receiver's expectations. For example, sending $\{N_A\}_{pk(B)}$ as a third message in the NS protocol, will be rejected by the responder, because it expects that it will receive an encrypted nonce which has a value equal to the one sent before.

To do that, we first define an enumerative domain, called *Type*, which contains the possible message's component types:

$$Type = \{ID, NC, PUBK, SECK, SHRK, ENCR, ANY\}$$

where *ID* is an identity, *NC* is a nonce, *PUBK* is a public key, *SECK* is a private key, *SHRK* is a shared key, *ENCR* is an encrypted component, and *ANY* is any component.

Next, we represent every message in a protocol as a syntax tree to capture the analysis performed by the intruder. By the analysis, we mean either decomposing the message into its components, or constructing a new message based on these components. The tree representation is supported by the following two definitions which are illustrated in Fig. 4.

Definition 1. *Let m be a message which is a sequence of components, then the syntactic tree of this message has the following properties:*

(1) its root is labelled with the message itself, while its other nodes are labelled with the message's sub components;

(2) a node in this tree, which is a sequence of more than one component, has a number of children;

(3) the node, which is a sequence of one encrypted component, has one child which is a sequence of its unencrypted components;

(4) its leaves are single sequences of unencrypted component;

(5) the root is numbered with a number equals to message number;

(6) the children for each node are assigned a left-to-right ordering numbers, started at 1.

Definition 2. *Let T_i be a tree for a message that has number i, $i = \{1, ..., n\}$. The position of the root node for T_i is a single sequence containing only i. The position of other nodes is the position of the parent node concatenated with the child order number for this node.*

The following step, based on the messages' tree representation, updates the intruder's knowledge with the eavesdropped messages, and generates the possible accepted messages. This step is detailed in the following subsections. Note that, the AsmetaL specifications for updating the intruder knowledge and generating the messages are available in [11].

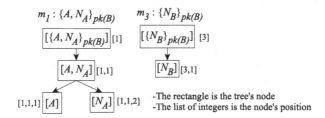

Fig. 4. Message tree representation examples for the NS protocol

3.2.1   Updating the Intruder's Knowledge. To save all the eavesdropped messages and their components, which are sequences of String, in the intruder knowledge, we define the function k: $Seq(Seq(String))$.

Typically, the $r\_UpdateTheKnowledge$ rule starts by saving the whole eavesdropped message in the k function. Then it saves each element of this message in k, and meanwhile checks whether the *type* of this element is encrypted, to decrypt it (if possible) and add the decrypted components to k. The type for each component is specified as a constant for our model by the static function *type: Prod(Protocol, Seq(Integer)) −> Type*. This function yields the type for the node that has a given position in a given protocol. For example, for the third message in NS protocol that has two nodes in its tree representation, we have the following $type(NS, [3]) = [ENCR]$, and $type(NS, [3, 1]) = [NC]$. While k is updated, the position of each node will be saved in the following function: *position: Prod(Seq(String), Integer, Integer)) −> Seq(Integer)*. This function permits easy access to the desired node of any message, by just giving the node's value, the session number, and the message number.

3.2.2   Generating Messages. We restrict the intruder's ability to generate messages by considering the type format of the message and its expected content. By type format, we mean the component types assumed by the receiver, e.g., for the second message in the NS protocol, the correct type format would be an encrypted message by a public key. While by the expected content, we mean the values of the components that the receiver would expect, e.g., the second message in addition to be encrypted under the receiver's public key, the value of the first component, which is a nonce, inside encryption must be equal to the nonce sent in the first message for NS protocol. Accordingly, we define the following static functions facilitating messages generation: (the first two functions are related to each node in the message's tree representation, while the rest are related to the encryption key)

(1) *type: Prod(Protocol, Seq(Integer))* $->$ *Type*: It is previously stated;
(2) *posExpVal: Prod(Protocol, Seq(Integer)* $->Seq(Integer)$: It returns the position of the expected value (if it exists) for the node that has a given position. For example, the nonce node of the third message for the NS protocol, which is at the [3, 1] position, has an expected value the same as that at [2, 1, 2] position, i.e., *posExpVal(NS, [3, 1])* = [2, 1, 2]. As a result, to generate the this message, the k sequence will be checked if it contains a node with a position returned by the *posExpVal* function.
(3) *posKeyId: Prod(Protocol, Seq(Integer)* $->Seq(Integer)$: It returns a specific identity for the key of the given encrypted component/node's position;
(4) *keyType: Prod(Protocol, Seq(Integer)* $->Seq(Type)$: It says what is the type of the key for the given encrypted component/node's position;
(5) *posKeyVal: Prod(Protocol, Seq(Integer)* $->Seq(Integer)$: It returns the expected key's position for the given position of the encrypted component.

Based on the all above functions, we specify the *r_GenerateMsg* rule for generating the potential accepted messages.

3.3 The Attack Scenarios Aspect

The attack scenarios concept is presented in [16], where five schemes of the origin and destination attacks from [25], including Man-in-the-Middle (MITM), Reflection (REFL), Denial of Service Replay (DoS_REPL), Simple Replay (Simple_REPL), and Interleaving (INTRL), have been defined. For each of the above schemes, a generic algorithm is designed, which when given parameters of the protocol, such as its steps number and sessions number, it will produce a scenario of an attack for this scheme. The algorithms also need to define an assignment of the participant's identity and the intruder impersonation to each role. At the beginning, the produced scenario is written in Common Syntax [9] and then is translated into an Estelle specification [7], to return the concrete simulated scenario. The honest participants and the intruder construct the messages in a scenario, but the intruder generates messages according to the component types.

In our work, we encode the attack scenarios directly into AsmetaL, and we restrict the messages generation action of the intruder with the expected message content and types as well. Our AsmetaL specification of a scenario for a given attack type, depends on the following static functions, that facilitate the assignment identification: *p: Prod(Integer, Integer, Task)* $->Id$, with *Task* = {*SENDER, RECEIVER*}, and *imp: Prod(Id, Integer)* $->Boolean$. The first function restores the identity for the given task: *SENDER, RECEIVER* for the participant's role at the given session and message numbers, while the second function says whether the given identity for a participant shared in a given session number is impersonated. Due to space restrictions, we present only the specification for the MITM attack scenario. The specifications for five scenarios are available in [11].

3.3.1 Man in the Middle (MITM) Attack Scenario. The MITM attack aims to secretly intercept, replay, alter messages between two participants and leaving them to believe that they are only communicating with each other. The scenario for this attack is laid out as follows: an odd message number is put in a sequence of session numbers arranged in the increasing order, while an even message number is put in a sequence of session numbers ordered in the decreasing order. For example, if we have 2 sessions and 3 messages, then the order of steps will be as follows: (1.1) (2.1) (2.2) (1.2) (1.3) (2.3). This scenario is built using one of the three possible assignments illustrated in Table 1.

Table 1. The possible assignments for MITM attack scenario

No	Odd sessions		Even sessions	
	Initiator	Responder	Initiator	Responder
1	A	I(B)	I(A)	B
2	A	I	I(A)	B
3	A	I(B)	I	B

```
rule r_ExchangeMsgs($p in Protocol)=              r_Responder[$p, $r]
let ($s=p(sNo, msgNo, SENDER)) in                endpar
let ($r=p(sNo, msgNo, RECEIVER))in              endif
  par                                           state:=SEND
    if state=SEND then                         endpar
      par                                      endif
        if $s=II or                          endpar
          imp($s, sNo, msgNo)=true then      endlet
            r_Intruder[NS]                  endlet
        else                              rule r_MITM_Scenario($p in Protocol)=
          par                             seq
            r_Initiator[$p, $s, $r]         stop:=totalSno
            r_Responder[$p, $s]             begin:=1
          endpar                            dir:=1
        endif                               while msgNo<=totalMsgNo and existAttack
        state:=RECEIVE                            =true do
      endpar                                  seq
    endif                                       while ((stop=totalSno and sNo<=stop)
    if state=RECEIVE then                          or (stop=1 and sNo>=stop)) and
      par                                        (existAttack=true) do
        if $r=II or                              r_ExchangeMsgs[$p]
          imp($r, sNo, msgNo)=true then        dir:=(-1)*dir
            par                                par
              r_UpdateTheKnowledge[$p]          stop:=begin
              sNo:=sNo+dir                      begin:=stop
            endpar                            endpar
        else                                  msgNo:=msgNo+1
          par                                 sNo:=begin
            r_Initiator[$p, $r, $s]         endseq
                                          endseq
```

Code 3: The r_ExchangeMsgs and the r_MITM_scenario rules

The AsmetaL specification for the MITM attack scenario is shown in the Code 3. In this Code, there are two rules: the *r_MITM_Scenario* rule, which models the scenario arrangement, and the *r_ExchangeMsgs* rule, which is called by the *r_MITM_Scenario* rule to send and receive a message by the participants. In *r_MITM_Scenario* rule, the *totalSno* function is a number of sessions, the *totalMsgNo* function is a number of messages, and *stop*, *begin*, and *dir* functions help achieving the increasing and decreasing order of the session's numbers.

In *r_ExchangeMsgs* rule, two situations are in parallel execution. First, when *state = SEND*, the *SENDER*'s identity is checked, if it is *II*, or it is impersonated, then the intruder will send a message. Otherwise, in parallel the *r_Initiator/r_Responder* rules are fired to send the current message by either the initiator or the responder depending on the *SENDER* identity of this message. Second, when *state = RECEIVE*, the *RECEIVER*'s identity is checked here, to either update the intruder's knowledge or to receive the current message by the initiator/responder. Sending a message by the intruder can be achieved by generating all the possible messages, and sending these messages one by one until one of them is accepted. If not, then there is no such attack scenario.

3.4   The Invariant Security Properties Aspect

In order to detect whether a protocol is vulnerable to an attack following a particular attack scenario, we use invariant checking for the security properties at simulated states of the protocol run. We are interested in inspecting two security constraints: *secrecy* and *authentication*.

Secrecy constraint is related to confirming that no secret information is obtained by others. For example, in NS protocol we have the following constraint:

invariant inv_sec over ncInt, k: not(contains(k, ncInt(AA, BB)))

It means that the intruder knowledge does not contain the nonce of *AA* which is sent to *BB*. The authentication property is defined in [26] based on the correspondence assertion style, as follows "when an authenticating principal finishes its part of the protocol, the authenticated principal must have been present and participated in its part of the protocol". This can be formulated as invariant constraint over *start* and *finish* functions, such as in NS protocol we have:

invariant inv_auth over start, finish: implies(finish(NS, 2, 1), start(NS, 2, 1))

It informally means that if a participant successfully finishes receiving the first message in the second session, then this implies that sending this message has been started previously in this session. Remember that the *start* and *finish* functions are updated only by the honest participants, not by the intruder.

4   Results and Discussion

Our experiments are concerned with simulating the protocol runs, which are specified by the attack scenario while observing the invariant properties. If there is no violation of any stated invariant property, there will be no successful attack related to these properties and the style of modelled attacks when its related scenario is simulated. In addition to the NS and TP protocols described in the background section, we have simulated three other protocols, including the Andrew

Secure RPC, the Denning Sacco (DS), and the Kehne Langendorfer Schoenwalder (KSL) [9].

By simulating the NS protocol using the MITM scenario with two sessions, we obtained four scenarios. Only one of them has messages that conform to the attack shown in Fig. 2b and its two invariant properties presented in Sect. 3.4 are violated. During this simulation, the intruder sends messages to honest participants three times. By the addition of the expected content check, the number of the generated messages each time is less than that obtained with the type matching method [16]. For example, in our method, the intruder generates 6 messages at the first step of second session: $\{A, N_A\}_{pk(B)}$, $\{B, N_A\}_{pk(B)}$, $\{I, N_A\}_{pk(B)}$, $\{A, N_I\}_{pk(B)}$, $\{B, N_I\}_{pk(B)}$, $\{I, N_I\}_{pk(B)}$. While 24 messages are generated based on the type matching method. Fewer messages are generated since the intruder is restricted with the expected responder public key, instead of all the known keys, including $pk(A), pk(B), pk(I), prk(I)$.

Note that, the attack scenarios give guidance exploring all runs with correct message formats and types while looking for attacks, and this can reduce the number of checked runs. As the number of protocol runs is positively impacted by the number of executed sessions and the number of steps in each session, reducing the generated messages by the intruder will eventually minimize the protocol runs. Combining the attack scenarios with the idea of reducing the intruder's messages can dramatically decrease the protocol runs.

Concerning the TP protocol, we obtain the attack in Fig. 3b and the attack in Fig. 3c by executing the MITM scenario with one session, and the REFL scenario with two sessions, respectively. In fact, our method is flexible in a way that it allows adding more checking abilities to the participants for easy detection of the attack in Fig. 3c by themselves, i.e., checking that the received message is not equal to the one sent in a session before. The TP protocol is a challenging case study as it's specification depends on the commutative encryption property. Commonly, this property is modelled as an equation directed from left to right (where the right-hand side is either a constant or a rigid subterm of the left-hand side) by tools like Proverif and Tamarin, in which case it can cause non-terminated analysis. We avoid this by modelling this property in a procedural way that captures the commutative equivalence condition.

Although understandably we cannot claim any form of completeness for our method, we can say that it detects attacks with given specified scenarios, including MITM, REFL, DoS_REPL, Simple_REPL, and INTRL, on protocols vulnerable to these attacks, though it cannot detect other attacks with undefined scenarios, such as type flaw attack.

5   Related Work

Different formal methods have been used for analysing security protocols. Model checking tools, such as Spin and NuSMV tools, have been applied to the automatic verification of security protocols, such as [3,19]. These tools successfully prove that insecure states are unreachable but with a bounding assumption for generated fresh components or protocol sessions.

With respect to the unbounded analysis issue, ProVerif [4], is a well-known tool that has emerged to address this. ProVerif employs Prolog style rules and executes an abstract representation technique to analyse an unbounded sessions. Its specification language is applied pi calculus. ProVerif reasonably proves secrecy and correspondence properties. However, for some protocols, e.g. TP protocol, and algebraic properties, ProVerif may go into an infinite loop which leads to a stack overflow. Recent work related to unbounded analysis [22], presents the Tamarin tool as a protocol verification tool in a symbolic model checking style. The specification language for Tamarin is based on multiset rewriting rules. Tamarin's language is more expressive than that of ProVerif in specifying security properties, as it supports direct modelling for temporal properties. It nevertheless shares with ProVerif the same non termination limitation.

The ASM method has been theoretically used for specifying and analysing security protocols, taking into account modelling intruder capabilities [1,2]. However, this work does not deal with expected content during generating messages.

The papers [17], and [16] are closest to our work. The first paper restricts the intruder's ability to generate only the messages of a particular type, which can be accepted by some agents. Depending only on type matching still may produce unacceptable messages. In [16] a methodology of simulating security protocols using scenarios designed for different attack schemes is presented. This is implemented in the Estelle language. The results showed it is an effective approach to reduce the number of protocol runs. However, in this work, the intruder generates messages based on method of [17]. In addition, this work does consider the algebraic properties of the encryption mechanism.

6 Conclusion

This paper follows the method in [16] to analyse security protocols using designed attack scenarios in a simulation based verification process. Our method differs from the [16] in three ways. First, the scenarios are specified in AsmetaL and simulated using AsmetaS tool. Second, we use two conditions: the expected message content and type matching, to limit the intruder's generated messages only to those that meet these conditions. Third, it deals with commutative encryption. Future research should consider the specification of scenarios for other attacks, such as a type-flaw attack.

Acknowledgments. A. Lisitsa and C. Dixon were partially supported by the EPSRC funded RAI Hub FAIR-SPACE (EP/R026092/1). F. Al-Shareefi was supported by the Higher Committee for Education Development in Iraq (HCED).

References

1. Bella, G., Riccobene, E.: Formal analysis of the Kerberos authentication system. J. Univers. Comput. Sci. **3**(12), 1337–1381 (1997)
2. Bella, G., Riccobene, E.: A realistic environment for crypto-protocol analyses by ASMs. In: Workshop on Abstract State Machines, pp. 127–138 (1998)

3. Ben Henda, N.: Generic and efficient attacker models in SPIN. In: SPIN Symposium on Model Checking of Software, pp. 77–86. ACM (2014)
4. Blanchet, B.: An efficient cryptographic protocol verifier based on Prolog rules. In: 14th IEEE Computer Security Foundations Workshop, pp. 82–96. IEEE (2001)
5. Börger, E., Raschke, A.: Modeling Companion for Software Practitioners. Springer, Heidelberg (2018). https://doi.org/10.1007/978-3-662-56641-1
6. Börger, E., Stärk, R.: Abstract State Machines: A Method Forhigh-level System Design and Analysis. Springer, Heidelberg (2003). https://doi.org/10.1007/978-3-642-18216-7
7. Budkowski, S., Dembinski, P.: An introduction to Estelle: a specification language for distributed systems. Comput. Netw. ISDN Syst. **14**(1), 3–23 (1987)
8. Carlsen, U.: Cryptographic protocol flaws: know your enemy. In: Proceedings the Computer Security Foundations Workshop VII, pp. 192–200. IEEE (1994)
9. Clark, J.A., Jacob, J.L.: A survey of authentication protocol literature. Technical report 1.0 (1997)
10. Dolev, D., Yao, A.: On the security of public key protocols. IEEE Trans. Inf. Theory **29**(2), 198–208 (1983)
11. Farah, A.S., Lisitsa, A., Clare, D.: The AsmetaL specifications for five security protocols and five attack scenarios. https://doi.org/10.5281/zenodo.2628743
12. Farahbod, R., Gervasi, V., Glässer, U.: CoreASM: an extensible ASM execution engine. Fund. Inform. **77**(1–2), 71–103 (2007)
13. Gargantini, A., Riccobene, E., Scandurra, P.: A metamodel-based language and a simulation engine for abstract state machines. J. UCS **14**(12), 1949–1983 (2008)
14. Gargantini, A., Riccobene, E., Scandurra, P.: Model-driven language engineering: The ASMETA case study. In: The Third International Conference on Software Engineering Advances. ICSEA, pp. 373–378. IEEE (2008)
15. Jacquemard, F.: Security protocols open repository (2003). http://www.lsv.ens-cachan.fr//spore/
16. Jakubowska, G., Dembiński, P., Penczek, W., Szreter, M.: Simulation of security protocols based on scenarios of attacks. Fund. Inform. **93**(1–3), 185–203 (2009)
17. Jakubowska, G., Penczek, W., Srebrny, M.: Verifying security protocols with timestamps via translation to timed automata. In: Proceedings of the International Workshop on Concurrency, Specification and Programming (CS&P 2005), pp. 100–115 (2005)
18. Lafourcade, P., Puys, M.: Performance evaluations of cryptographic protocols verification tools dealing with algebraic properties. In: Garcia-Alfaro, J., Kranakis, E., Bonfante, G. (eds.) FPS 2015. LNCS, vol. 9482, pp. 137–155. Springer, Cham (2016). https://doi.org/10.1007/978-3-319-30303-1_9
19. Lomuscio, A., Pecheur, C., Raimondi, F.: Automatic verification of knowledge and time with NuSMV. In: Proceedings of the Twentieth International Joint Conference on Artificial Intelligence, pp. 1384–1389. IJCAI/AAAI Press (2007)
20. Lowe, G.: An attack on the needham-schroeder public-key authentication protocol. Inf. Process. Lett. **56**(3), 131–132 (1995)
21. Massey, J.L.: An introduction to contemporary cryptology. Proc. IEEE **76**(5), 533–549 (1988)
22. Meier, S., Schmidt, B., Cremers, C., Basin, D.: The TAMARIN prover for the symbolic analysis of security protocols. In: Sharygina, N., Veith, H. (eds.) CAV 2013. LNCS, vol. 8044, pp. 696–701. Springer, Heidelberg (2013). https://doi.org/10.1007/978-3-642-39799-8_48
23. Needham, R.M., Schroeder, M.D.: Using encryption for authentication in large networks of computers. Commun. ACM **21**(12), 993–999 (1978)

24. Shamir, A., Rivest, R.L., Adleman, L.M.: Mental poker. Technical report TM-125, MIT Laboratry for Computer Science (1978)
25. Syverson, P.: A taxonomy of replay attacks. In: Computer Security Foundations Workshop VII (CSFW 1994), pp. 187–191. IEEE (1994)
26. Woo, T.Y., Lam, S.S.: A semantic model for authentication protocols. In: Proceedings of the 1993 IEEE Computer Society Symposium on Research in Security and Privacy, 1993, pp. 178–194. IEEE (1993)

Running on Fumes
Preventing Out-of-Gas Vulnerabilities in Ethereum Smart Contracts Using Static Resource Analysis

Elvira Albert[1], Pablo Gordillo[1(✉)], Albert Rubio[1], and Ilya Sergey[2]

[1] Complutense University of Madrid, Madrid, Spain
pabgordi@ucm.es
[2] Yale-NUS College and School of Computing, NUS, Singapore, Singapore

Abstract. Gas is a measurement unit of the computational effort that it will take to execute every single operation that takes part in the Ethereum blockchain platform. Each instruction executed by the Ethereum Virtual Machine (EVM) has an associated gas consumption specified by Ethereum. If a transaction exceeds the amount of gas allotted by the user (known as gas limit), an *out-of-gas* exception is raised. There is a wide family of contract vulnerabilities due to *out-of-gas* behaviors. We report on the design and implementation of GASTAP, a Gas-Aware Smart contracT Analysis Platform, which takes as input a smart contract (either in EVM, disassembled EVM, or in Solidity source code) and automatically infers gas upper bounds for all its public functions. Our bounds ensure that if the gas limit paid by the user is higher than our inferred gas bounds, the contract is free of out-of-gas vulnerabilities.

1 Introduction

In the Ethereum consensus protocol, every operation on a replicated blockchain state, which can be performed in a transactional manner by executing a *smart contract* code, costs a certain amount of *gas* [29], a monetary value in *Ether*, Ethereum's currency, paid by a transaction-proposing party. Computations (performed by invoking smart contracts) that require *more computational or storage resources*, cost more gas than those that require fewer resources. As regards storage, the EVM has three areas where it can store items: the *storage* is where all *contract state* variables reside, every contract has its own storage and it is persistent between external function calls (transactions) and quite expensive to use; the *memory* is used to hold temporary values, and it is erased between transactions and is cheaper to use; the *stack* is used to carry out operations and it is free to use, but can only hold a limited amount of values.

This work was funded partially by the Spanish MINECO project TIN2015-69175-C4-2-R and MINECO/FEDER, UE project TIN2015-69175-C4-3-R, by Spanish MICINN/FEDER, UE projects RTI2018-094403-B-C31 and RTI2018-094403-B-C33, by the CM project S2018/TCS-4314 and by the UCM CT27/16-CT28/16 grant.

© Springer Nature Switzerland AG 2019
P. Ganty and M. Kaâniche (Eds.): VECoS 2019, LNCS 11847, pp. 63–78, 2019.
https://doi.org/10.1007/978-3-030-35092-5_5

The rationale behind the resource-aware smart contract semantics, instrumented with gas consumption, is three-fold. First, paying for gas at the moment of proposing the transaction does not allow the emitter to waste other parties' (aka *miners*) computational power by requiring them to perform a lot of worthless intensive work. Second, gas fees disincentivize users to consume too much of replicated *storage*, which is a valuable resource in a blockchain-based consensus system. Finally, such a semantics puts a cap on the number of computations that a transaction can execute, hence prevents attacks based on non-terminating executions (which could otherwise, *e.g.*, make all miners loop forever).

In general, the gas-aware operational semantics of EVM has introduced novel challenges *wrt.* sound static reasoning about resource consumption, correctness, and security of replicated computations: (1) While the EVM specification [29] provides the precise gas consumption of the low-level operations, most of the smart contracts are written in high-level languages, such as Solidity [13] or Vyper [14]. The translation of the high-level language constructs to the low-level ones makes static estimation of runtime gas bounds challenging (as we will see throughout this paper), and is implemented in an *ad-hoc* way by state-of-the art compilers, which are only able to give constant gas bounds, or return ∞ otherwise. (2) As noted in [17], it is discouraged in the Ethereum safety recommendations [16] that the gas consumption of smart contracts depends on the size of the data it stores (i.e., the *contract state*), as well as on the size of its functions inputs, or of the current state of the blockchain. However, according to our experiments, almost 10% of the functions we have analyzed do. The inability to estimate those dependencies, and the lack of analysis tools, leads to design mistakes, which make a contract unsafe to run or prone to exploits. For instance, a contract whose state size exceeds a certain limit, can be made forever *stuck*, not being able to perform any operation within a reasonable gas bound. Those vulnerabilities have been recognized before, but only discovered by means of unsound, pattern-based analysis [17].

In this paper, we address these challenges in a principled way by developing GASTAP, a *Gas-Aware Smart contracT Analysis Platform*, which is, to the best of our knowledge, the first automatic gas analyzer for smart contracts. GASTAP takes as input a smart contract provided in Solidity source code [13], or in low-level (possibly decompiled [26]) EVM code, and automatically infers an upper bound on the gas consumption for each of its public functions. The upper bounds that GASTAP infers are given in terms of the sizes of the input parameters of the functions, the contract state, and/or on the blockchain data that the gas consumption depends upon (e.g., on the *Ether* value).

The inference of gas requires complex transformation and analysis processes on the code that include: (1) construction of the control-flow graphs (CFGs), (2) decompilation from low-level code to a higher-level representation, (3) inference of size relations, (4) generation of gas equations, and (5) solving the equations into closed-form gas bounds. Therefore, building an automatic gas analyzer from EVM code requires a daunting implementation effort that has been possible thanks to the availability of a number of existing open-source tools that we have succeeded to extend and put together in the GASTAP system. In particular, an extension of the tool OYENTE [3] is used for (1), an improved representation of

ETHIR [6] is used for (2), an adaptation of the size analyzer of SACO [4] is used to infer the size relations, and the PUBS [5] solver for (5).

The most challenging aspect in the design of GASTAP has been the approximation of the EVM gas model (which is formally specified in [29]) that is required to produce the gas equations in step (4). This is because the EVM gas model is highly complex and unconventional. The gas consumption of each instruction has two parts: (i) the *memory gas cost*, if the instruction accesses a location in memory which is beyond the previously accessed locations (known as *active* memory [29]), it pays a gas proportional to the distance of the accessed location. (ii) The second part, the *opcode gas cost*, is related to the bytecode instruction itself. This component is also complex to infer because it is not always a constant amount, it might depend in some cases on the current global and local state.

GASTAP has a wide range of applications for contract developers, attackers and owners, including the detection of vulnerabilities, debugging and verification/certification of gas usage. As contract developers and owners, having a precise resource analyzer allows answering the following query about a specific smart contract: "what is the amount of gas necessary to *safely* (i.e., without an out-of-gas exception) reach a certain execution point in the contract code, or to execute a function"? This can be used for debugging, verifying/certifying a safe amount of gas for running, as well as ensuring progress conditions. Besides, GASTAP allows us to calculate the safe amount of gas that one should provide to an external data source (e.g., contracts using Oraclize [8]) in order to enable a successful callback. As an attacker, one might estimate, how much *Ether* (in gas), an adversary has to pour into a contract in order to execute the DoS attack. We note that such an attack may, however, be economically impractical.

Finally, we argue that our experimental evaluation shows that GASTAP is an effective and efficient tool: we have analyzed more than 29,000 real smart contracts pulled from etherscan.io [2], that in total contain 258,541 public functions, and inferred gas bounds for 91.85% of them in 342.54 h. GASTAP can be used from a web interface at https://costa.fdi.ucm.es/gastap.

2   Description of GASTAP Components

Figure 1 depicts the architecture of GASTAP. In order to describe all components of our tool, we use as running example a simplified version (without calls to the external service Oraclize and the authenticity proof verifier) of the EthereumPot contract [1] that implements a simple lottery. During a game, players call a method joinPot to buy lottery tickets; each player's address is appended to an array addresses of current players, and the number of tickets is appended to an array slots, both having variable length. After some time has elapsed, anyone can call rewardWinner which calls the Oraclize service to obtain a random number for the winning ticket. If all goes according to plan, the Oraclize service then responds by calling the __callback method with this random number and the authenticity proof as arguments. A new instance of the game is then started, and the winner is allowed to withdraw her balance using a withdraw method. In Fig. 2, an excerpt of the Solidity code (including the public function findWinner)

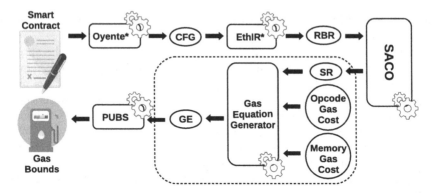

Fig. 1. Architecture of GASTAP (CFG: control flow graph; RBR: rule-based representation; SR: size-relations; GE: gas equations)

and a fragment of the EVM code produced by the compiler, are displayed. The Solidity source code is showed for readability, as GASTAP analyzes directly the EVM code (if it receives the source, it first compiles it to obtain the EVM code).

2.1 Oyente*: From EVM to a Complete CFG

The first component of our tool, OYENTE*, is an extension of the open-source tool OYENTE [3], a symbolic execution tool developed to analyze Ethereum smart contracts and find potential security bugs. As OYENTE's aim is on symbolic execution rather than on generating a complete CFG, some extensions are needed to this end. The ETHIR framework [6] had already extended OYENTE for two purposes: (1) to recover the list of addresses for unconditional blocks with more than one possible jump address (as OYENTE originally only kept the last processed one), and (2) to add more explicit information to the CFG: jump operations are decorated with the jumping address, discovered by OYENTE, and, other operations like store or load are also decorated with the address they operate: the number of state variable for operations on storage; and the memory location for operations on memory if OYENTE is able to discover it (or with "?" otherwise).

However ETHIR's extension still produced incomplete CFGs. OYENTE* further extends it to handle a more subtle source of incompleteness in the generated CFG that comes directly from the fact that OYENTE is a symbolic execution engine. For symbolic execution, a bound on the number of times a loop is iterated is given. Hence it may easily happen that some (feasible) paths are not reached in the exploration within this bound and they are lost. To solve this problem, we have modified OYENTE to remove the execution bound (as well as other checks that were only used for their particular applications), and have added information to the path under analysis. Namely, every time a new jump is found, we check if the jumping point is already present in the path. In such case, an edge to that point is added and the exploration of the trace is stopped. As a side effect, we not only produce a complete CFG, but also avoid much useless exploration for our purposes which results in important efficiency gain.

```
contract EthereumPot {                                      ...
  address[] public addresses;                               DUP1
  address public winnerAddress;                             PUSH1 => 0x00
  uint[] public slots;                                      SWAP1
  ...                                                        POP
  function __callback(bytes32 _queryId, string _result , bytes _proof)    PUSH1 => 0x03
    oraclize_randomDS_proofVerify(_queryId, _result, _proof) {            DUP1
    if(msg.sender != oraclize_cbAddress()) throw;            SLOAD
    random_number = uint(sha3(_result))                     SWAP1
    winnerAddress = findWinner(random_number);              ...
    amountWon = this.balance * 98 / 100 ;                   PUSH1 => 0x40
    winnerAnnounced(winnerAddress, amountWon);              MLOAD
    if(winnerAddress.send(amountWon)) {                     DUP1
      if(owner.send(this.balance)) {                        SWAP2
        openPot();                                          SUB
      }}                                                    SWAP1
    }                                                       SHA3
  function findWinner(uint random) constant returns(address winner){   PUSH1 => 0x01
    for(uint i = 0; i < slots.length; i++) {                ...
      if(random <= slots[i]) {                              JUMPDEST
        return addresses[i];                                MOD
      }}                                                    ADD
    }                                                       PUSH1 => 0x0a
  ...                                                        DUP2
}                                                           SWAP1
                                                            SSTORE
                                                            POP
                                                            PUSH2 => 0x0954
                                                            PUSH1 => 0x0a
                                                            SLOAD
                                                            PUSH2 => 0x064b
                                                            JUMP
                                                            ...
```

Fig. 2. Excerpt of Solidity code for `EthereumPot` contract (left), and fragment of EVM code for function `__callback` (right)

When applying OYENTE*, our extended/modified version of OYENTE, we obtain a *complete* CFG, with the additional annotations already provided by [6].

2.2 EthIR*: From CFG to an Annotated Rule-Based Representation

ETHIR*, an extension of ETHIR [6], is the next component of our analyzer. ETHIR provides a rule-based representation (RBR) for the CFG obtained from OYENTE*. Intuitively, for each block in the CFG it generates a corresponding rule that contains a high-level representation of all bytecode instructions in the block (e.g., load and store operations are represented as assignments) and that has as parameters an explicit representation of the stack, local, state, and blockchain variables (details of the transformation are in [6]). Conditional branching in the CFG is represented by means of guards in the rules. ETHIR* provides three extensions to the original version of ETHIR [6]: (1) The first extension is related to the way function calls are handled in the EVM, where instead of an explicit CALL opcode, as we have seen before, a call to an internal function is transformed into a PUSH of the return address in the stack followed by a JUMP to the address where the code of the function starts. If the same function is called from different points of the program, the resulting CFG shares for all these calls the same subgraph (the one representing the code of the function) which ends with different jumping addresses at the end. As described in [17], there is a need to clone parts of the CFG to explicitly link the PUSH of the return address with the final JUMP to this address. This cloning in our implementation is done at the level of the RBR as follows: Since the jumping addresses are known thanks to the symbolic execution applied by OYENTE, we can find the connection between the PUSH and the JUMP and clone the involved part of the

RBR (between the rule of the PUSH and of the JUMP) using different rule names
for each cloning. (2) The second extension is a flow analysis intended to reduce
the number of parameters of the rules of the RBR. This is crucial for efficiency
as the number of involved parameters is a bottleneck for the successive analysis
steps that we are applying. Basically, before starting the translation phase, we
compute the inverse connected component for each block of the CFG, i.e, the
set of its predecessor blocks. During the generation of each rule, we identify the
local, state or blockchain variables that are used in the body of the rule. Then,
these variables have to be passed as arguments only to those rules built from
the blocks of its inverse connected component. (3) When we find a store on an
unknown memory location "?", we have to "forget" all the memory from that
point on, since the writing may affect any memory location, and it is not sound
anymore to assume the previous information. In the RBR, we achieve this dele-
tion by assigning fresh variables (thus unknown values) to the memory locations
at this point.

Optionally, ETHIR provides in the RBR the original bytecode instructions
(from which the higher-level ones are obtained) by simply wrapping them within
a nop functor (see Fig. 3). Although nop annotations will be ignored by the size
analysis, they are needed later to assign a precise gas consumption to every rule.

$$
\begin{aligned}
&block1647(\overline{s_{10}}, \overline{sv}, \overline{lv}, \overline{bc}) \Rightarrow \\
&\quad nop(JUMPDEST), s_{11} = s_9, s_9 = s_{10}, s_{10} = s_{11}, nop(SWAP), s_{11} = 0, nop(PUSH), \\
&\quad l_2 = s_{10}, nop(MSTORE), s_{10} = 32, nop(PUSH), s_{11} = 0, nop(PUSH), s_{10} = sha3(s_{11}, s_{10}), \\
&\quad nop(SHA3), s_9 = s_{10} + s_9, nop(ADD), gl = s_9, s_9 = fresh_0, nop(SLOAD), s_{10} = s_6, \\
&\quad nop(DUP4), call(jump1647(\overline{s_{10}}, \overline{sv}, \overline{lv}, \overline{bc})), nop(GT), nop(ISZERO), nop(ISZERO), \\
&\quad nop(PUSH), nop(JUMPI)
\end{aligned}
$$

Fig. 3. Selected rule including nop functions needed for gas analysis

Example 1. Figure 3 shows the RBR for *block1647*. Bytecode instructions that
load or store information are transformed into assignments on the involved variables. For arithmetic operations, operations on bits, sha, etc., the variables they
operate on are made explicit. Since stack variables are always consecutive we
denote by $\overline{s_n}$ the decreasing sequence of all s_i form n down to 0. $\overline{lv}$ includes l_2
and l_0, which is the subset of the local variables that are needed in this rule or
in further calls (second extension of ETHIR*). The unknown location "?" has
become a fresh variable $fresh_0$ in *block1647*. For state variables, $\overline{sv}$ includes the
needed ones $g_{11}, g_8, g_7, g_6, g_5, g_3, g_2, g_1, g_0$ (g_i is the i-th state variable). Finally,
$\overline{bc}$ includes the needed blockchain state variables address, balance and timestamp.

2.3   SACO: Size Relations for EVM Smart Contracts

In the next step, we generate *size relations* (SR) from the RBR using the SACO
tool [4]. SR are equations and inequations that state how the sizes of data change
in the rule [12]. This information is obtained by analyzing how each instruction of
the rules modifies the sizes of the data it uses, and propagating this information
as usual in dataflow analysis. SR are needed to build the gas equations and then
generate gas bounds in the last step of the process. The size analysis of SACO
has been slightly modified to ignore the *nop* instructions. Besides, before sending

the rules to SACO, we replace the instructions that cannot be handled (e.g., bit-wise operations, hashes) by assignments with fresh variables (to represent an unknown value). Apart from this, we are able to adjust our representation to make use of the approach followed by SACO, which is based on abstracting data (structures) to their sizes. For integer variables, the size abstraction corresponds to their value and thus it works directly. However, a language specific aspect of this step is the handling of data structures like array, string or bytes (an array of byte). In the case of array variables, SACO's size analysis works directly as in EVM the slot assigned to the variable contains indeed its length (and the address where the array content starts is obtained with the hash of the slot address).

Example 2. Consider the following SR (those in brackets) generated for rule *jump1649* and *block1731*:

$jump1619(\overline{s_{10}}, \overline{sv}, \overline{lv}, \overline{bc}) = block1633(\overline{s_8}, \overline{sv}, \overline{lv}, \overline{bc})\{s_{10} < s_9\}$

$block1731(\overline{s_8}, \overline{sv}, \overline{lv}, \overline{bc}) = 41 + block1619(s_8', \overline{s_7}, \overline{sv}, \overline{lv}, \overline{bc})\{s_8' = 1 + s_8\}$

The size relations for the *jump1619* function involve the `slots` array length (g_3 stored in s_9) and the local variable i (in s_8 and copied to s_{10}). It corresponds to the guard of the `for` loop in function `findWinner` that compares i and `slots.length` and either exits the loop or iterates (and hence consume different amount of gas). The size relation on s_8 for *block1731* corresponds to the size increase in the loop counter.

However, for bytes and string it is more challenging, as the way they are stored depends on their actual sizes. Roughly, if they are short (at most 31 bytes long) their data is stored in the same slot together with its length. Otherwise, the slot contains the length (and the address where the string or bytes content starts is obtained like for arrays). Our approach to handle this issue is as follows. In the presence of bytes or string, we can find in the rules of the RBR a particular sequence of instructions (which are always the same) that start pushing the contents of the string or bytes variable in the top of the stack, obtain its length, and leave it stored in the top of the stack (at the same position). Therefore, to avoid losing information, since SACO is abstracting the data structures to their sizes, every time we find this pattern of instructions applied to a string or bytes variable, we just remove them from the RBR (keeping the nops to account for their gas). Importantly, since the top of the stack has indeed the size, under SACO's abstraction it is equal to the string or bytes variable. Being precise, assuming that we have placed the contents of the string or bytes variable in the top of the stack, which is s_i, the transformation applied is the following:

$s_{i+1} = 1, nop(PUSH1), s_{i+2} = s_i, nop(DUP2), s_{i+3} = 1, nop(PUSH1),$
$s_{i+2} = and(s_{i+3}, s_{i+2}), nop(AND), s_{i+2} = eq(s_{i+2}, 0), nop(ISZERO),$
$s_{i+3} = 256, nop(PUSH2), s_{i+2} = s_{i+3} * s_{i+2}, nop(MUL), s_{i+1} = s_{i+2} - s_{i+1},$
$nop(SUB)s_i = and(s_{i+1}, s_i), nop(AND), s_{i+1} = 2, nop(PUSH1),$
$s_{i+2} = s_i, s_i = s_{i+1}, s_{i+1} = s_{i+2}, nop(SWAP1), s_i = s_{i+1}/s_i, nop(DIV)$

$\Downarrow$

$nop(PUSH1), nop(DUP2), nop(PUSH1), nop(AND), nop(ISZERO), nop(PUSH2),$
$nop(MUL), nop(SUB), nop(AND), nop(PUSH1), nop(SWAP1), nop(DIV)$

Since the involved instructions include bit-wise operations among others and, as said, the value of the stack variable becomes unknown, without this transformation the relation between the stack variable and the length of the string or bytes would be lost and, as a result, the tool may fail to provide a bound on the gas consumption. This transformation is applied when possible and, e.g., is needed to infer bounds for the functions `getPlayers` and `getSlots` (see Table 2).

2.4   Generation of Equations

In order to generate gas equations (GE), we need to define the EVM gas model, which is obtained by encoding the specification of the gas consumption for each EVM instruction as provided in [29]. The EVM gas model is complex and unconventional, it has two components, one which is related to the memory consumption, and another one that depends on the bytecode executed. The first component is computed separately as will be explained below. In this section we focus on computing the gas attributed to the opcodes. For this purpose, we provide a function $C_{opcode} : s \mapsto g$ which, for an EVM opcode, takes a stack s and returns a gas g associated to it. We distinguish three types of instructions: (1) Most bytecode instructions have a *fixed* constant gas consumption that we encode precisely in the cost model C_{opcode}, i.e., g is a constant. (2) Bytecode instructions that have different *constant* gas consumption g_1 or g_2 depending on some given condition. This is the case of `SSTORE` that costs $g_1 = 20000$ if the storage value is set from zero to non-zero (first assignment), and $g_2 = 5000$ otherwise. But it is also the case for `CALL` and `SELFDESTRUCT`. In these cases we use $g = max(g_1, g_2)$ in C_{opcode}. (3) Bytecode instructions with a non-constant (*parametric*) gas consumption that depends on the value of some stack location. For instance, the gas consumption of `EXP` is defined as $10 + 10 \cdot (1 + \lfloor log_{256}(\mu_s[1]) \rfloor)$ if $\mu_s[1] \neq 0$ where $\mu_s[0]$ is the top of the stack. Therefore, we have to define g in C_{opcode} as a parametric function that uses the involved location. Other bytecode instructions with parametric cost are `CALLDATACOPY`, `CODECOPY`, `RETURNDATACOPY`, `CALL`, `SHA3`, `LOG*`, and `EXTCODECOPY`.

Given the RBR annotated with the nop information, the size relations, and the cost model C_{opcode}, we can generate GE that define the gas consumption of the corresponding code applying the classical approach to cost analysis [28] which consists of the following basic steps: (i) Each rule is transformed into a corresponding cost equation that defines its cost. Example 2 also displays the GE obtained for the rules *jump1619* and *block1731*. (ii) The nop instructions determine the gas that the rule consumes according to the gas cost model C_{opcode} explained above. (iii) Calls to other rules are replaced by calls to the corresponding cost equations. See for instance the call to *block1619* from rule *block1731* that is transformed into a call to the cost function *block1619* in Example 2. (iv) Size relations are attached to rules to define their applicability conditions and how the sizes of data change when the equation is applied. See for instance the size relations attached to *jump1619* that have been explained in Example 2.

As said before, the gas model includes a cost that comes from the memory consumption which is as follows. Let $C_{mem}(a)$ be the memory cost function for a given memory slot a and defined as $G_{memory} \cdot a + \left\lfloor \frac{a^2}{512} \right\rfloor$ where $G_{memory} = 3$. Given an EVM instruction, μ_i' and μ_i denote resp. the *highest memory slot* accessed in the local memory, resp., after and before the execution of such instruction. The memory gas cost of every instruction is the difference $C_{mem}(\mu_i') - C_{mem}(\mu_i)$. Besides MLOAD or MSTORE, instructions like SHA3 or CALL, among others, make use of the local memory, and hence can increase the memory gas cost.

In order to estimate this cost associated to all EVM instructions in the code of the function, we first make the following observations: (1) Computing the sum of all the memory gas cost amounts to computing the memory cost function for the highest memory slot accessed by the instructions of the function under analysis. This is because, as seen, μ_i and μ_i' refer to this position in each operation and hence we pay for all the memory up to this point. (2) This is not a standard memory consumption analysis in which one obtains the total amount of memory allocated by the function. Instead, in this case, we infer the actual value of the highest slot accessed by any operation executed in the function.

Example 3. Let us show how we obtain the memory gas cost for *block1647*. In this case, the two instructions in this block that cost memory are underlined in Fig. 3 and correspond to a MSTORE and SHA3 bytecodes. In this block, both bytecodes operate on slot 0 of the memory, and they cost 3 units of gas because they only activate up to slot 1 of the memory.

2.5 PUBS Solver: From Equations to Closed-Form Bounds

The last step of the gas bounds inference is the generation of a *closed-form gas upper bound*, i.e., a solution for the GE as a non-recursive expression. As the GE we have generated have the standard form of cost relations systems, they can be solved using off-the-shelf solvers, such as Pubs [5] or Cofloco [15], without requiring any modification. These systems are able to find polynomial, logarithmic and exponential solutions for cost relations in a fully automatic way. The gas bounds computed for all public functions of EthereumPot using Pubs can be found in Table 1, note that they are parametric on different state variables, input and blockchain data.

3   Experimental Evaluation

This section presents the results of our evaluation of Gastap. In Sect. 3.1, we evaluate the accuracy of the gas bounds inferred by Gastap on the EthereumPot by comparing them with the bounds computed by the Solidity compiler.

In Sect. 3.2, we evaluate the efficiency and effectiveness of our tool by analyzing more than 29,000 Ethereum smart contracts. To obtain these contracts, we pulled from etherscan.io [2] all Ethereum contracts whose source code was available on January 2018. Gastap is available at https://costa.fdi.ucm.es/gastap.

3.1   Gas Bounds for **EthereumPot** Case Study

Table 1 shows in column **solc** the gas bound provided by the Solidity compiler **solc** [13], and in the next two columns the bounds produced by GASTAP for opcode gas and memory gas, respectively, for all public functions in the contract. If we add the gas and memory bounds, it can be observed that, for those functions with constant gas consumption, we are as accurate as **solc**. Hence, we do not lose precision due to the use of static analysis.

For those 6 functions that **solc** fails to infer constant gas consumption, it returns ∞. For opcode gas, we are able to infer precise *parametric* bounds for five of them, **rewardWinner** is linear on the size of the first and third state variables ($g1$ and $g3$ represent resp. the sizes of the arrays **addresses** and **slots** in Fig. 2), **getSlots** and **findWinner** on the third, **getPlayers** on the first, and **__callback** besides depends on the value of **result** (second function parameter) and **proof** (last parameter). It is important to note that, although the Solidity source code of some functions (*e.g.*, of **getSlots** and **getPlayers**) does not contain loops, they are generated by the compiler and are only visible at the EVM level. This also happens, for example, when a function takes a *string* or *bytes* variable as argument. This shows the need of developing the gas analyzer at the EVM level.

For **joinPot** we cannot ensure that the gas consumption is finite without embedding information about the blockchain in the analyzer. This is because **joinPot** has a loop: for (**uint** i = msg.value; i >= minBetSize; i-= minBetSize) {tickets++;}, where **minBetSize** is a state variable that is initialized in the definition line as **uint minBetSize** = 0.01ether, and **ether** is the value of the *Ether* at the time of executing the instruction. This code has indeed several problems. The first one is that the initialization of the state variable **minBetSize** to the value 0.01ether does not appear in the EVM code available in the blockchain. This is because this instruction is executed only once when the contract is created. So our analyzer cannot find this instruction and the value of **minBetSize** is unknown (and hence no bound can be found). Besides, the loop indeed does not terminate if **minBetSize** in not strictly greater than zero (which could indeed happen if **ether** would take zero or a negative value). If we add the initialization instruction, and embed in the analyzer the invariant that **ether** > 0 (hence **minBetSize** becomes > 0), then we are able to infer a bound for **joinPot**.

For **__callback** we guarantee that the memory gas is *finite* but we cannot obtain an upper bound for it, GASTAP yields a *maximization error* which is a consequence of the information loss due to the soundness requirement described in extension 3 of Sect. 2.2. Intuitively, maximization errors may occur when the analyzer needs to compose the cost of the different fragments of the code. For the composition, it needs to maximize (*i.e.*, find the maximal value) the cost of inner components in their calling contexts (see [5] for details). If the maximization process involves memory locations that have been "forgotten" by ETHIR* (variables "?"), the upper bound cannot be inferred. Still, if there is no ranking function error, we know that all loops terminate, thus the memory gas consumption is finite.

Table 1. Gas bounds for `EthereumPot`. Function `nat` defined as `nat(l)=max(0,l)`.

function	solc	opcode bound GASTAP	memory bound GASTAP
`totalBet`	790	775	15
`locked`	706	691	15
`getEndTime`	534	519	15
`slots`	837	822	15
`rewardWinner`	∞	$80391+5057\cdot\text{nat}(g3)+5057\cdot\text{nat}(g1)$	18
`Kill`	30883	30874	9
`amountWon`	438	423	15
`getPlayers`	∞	$1373+292\cdot\text{nat}(g1-1/32)$ $+75\cdot\text{nat}(g1+31/32)$	$6\cdot\text{nat}(g1)+24+\left\lfloor\frac{(6\cdot nat(g1)+24)^2}{512}\right\rfloor$
`getSlots`	∞	$1507+250\cdot\text{nat}(g3-1/32)$ $+75\cdot\text{nat}(g3+31/32)$	$6\cdot\text{nat}(g3)+24+\left\lfloor\frac{(6\cdot nat(g3)+24)^2}{512}\right\rfloor$
`winnerAddress`	750	735	15
`__callback`	∞	$229380+3\cdot(\text{nat}(\text{proof})/32)$ $+103\cdot\text{nat}(\text{result}/32)$ $+50\cdot\text{nat}((32-\text{nat}(\text{result})))$ $+5836\cdot\text{nat}(g3)+5057\cdot\text{nat}(g1)$	max_error
`owner`	662	647	15
`endTime`	460	445	15
`potTime`	746	731	15
`potSize`	570	555	15
`joinPot`	∞	no_rf	9
`addresses`	1116	1101	15
`findWinner`	∞	$1555+779\cdot\text{nat}(g3)$	15
`random_number`	548	533	15

Finally, this transaction is called always with a constant gas limit of 400,000. This contrasts with the non-constant gas bound obtained using GASTAP. Note that if the gas spent (without including the *refunds*) goes beyond the gas limit the transaction ends with an out-of-gas exception. Since the size of $g3$ and $g1$ is the same as the number of players, from our bound, we can conclude that from 16 players on the contract is in risk of running out-of-gas and get stuck as the 400,000 gas limit cannot be changed. So using GASTAP we can prevent an out-of-gas vulnerability: the contract should not allow more than 15 players, or the gas limit must be increased from that number on.

3.2 Statistics for Analyzed Contracts

Our experimental setup consists on 29,061 contracts taken from the blockchain as follows. We pulled all Ethereum contracts from the blockchain as of January 2018, and removed duplicates. This ended up in 10,796 files (each file often contains several contracts). We have excluded the files where the decompilation phase fails in any of the contracts it includes, since in that case we do not get any information on the whole file. This failure is due to OYENTE in 1,230 files, which represents a 11.39% of the total and to ETHIR in 829 files, which represents a 7.67% of the total. The failures of ETHIR are mainly due to the cloning mechanism in involved CFGs for which we fail to find the relation between the jump instruction and the return address.

After removing these files, our experimental evaluation has been carried out on the remaining 8,737 files, containing 29,061 contracts. In total we have analyzed 258,541 public functions (and all auxiliary functions that are used from them). Experiments have been performed on an Intel Core i7-7700T at 2.9 GHz x 8 and 7.7 GB of Memory, running Ubuntu 16.04. GASTAP accepts smart contracts written in versions of Solidity up to 0.4.25 or bytecode for the Ethereum Virtual Machine v1.8.18. The statistics that we have obtained in number of functions are summarized in Table 2, and the time taken by the analyzer in Table 3. The results for the opcode and memory gas consumption are presented separately.

Table 2. Statistics of gas usage on the analyzed 29,061 smart contracts from Ethereum blockchain

Type of result	#opc	%opc	#mem	%mem
Constant gas bound	223,294	86.37%	225,860	87.36%
Parametric gas bound	14,167	5.48%	13,312	5.15%
Time out	13,140	5.08%	13,539	5.24%
Finite gas bound (maximization error)	7,095	2.74%	5,830	2.25%
Termination unknown (ranking function error)	716	0.28%	0	0%
Complex control flow (cover point error)	129	0.05%	0	0%
Total number of functions	258,541	100%	258,541	100%

Let us first discuss the results in Table 2 which aim at showing the effectiveness of GASTAP. Columns **#opc** and **#mem** contain number of analyzed functions for opcode and memory gas, resp., and columns preceded by % the percentage they represent. For the analyzed contracts, we can see that a large number of functions, 86.37% (resp. 87.36%), have a constant opcode (resp. memory) gas consumption. This is as expected because of the nature of smart contracts, as well as because of the Ethereum safety recommendations mentioned in Sect. 1. Still, there is a relevant number of functions 5.48% (resp. 5.15%) for which we obtain an opcode (resp. memory) gas bound that is not constant (and hence are potentially vulnerable). Additionally, 5.08% of the analyzed functions for opcodes and 5.24% for memory reach the timeout (set to 1 min) due to the further complexity of solving the equations.

As the number of analyzed contracts is very large, a manual inspection of all of them is not possible. Having inspected many of them and, thanks to the information provided by the PUBS solver used by GASTAP, we are able to classify the types of errors that have led to a *"don't-know"* answer and which in turn explain the sources of incompleteness by our analysis: (i) *Maximization error*: In many cases, a *maximization error* is a consequence of loss of information by the size analysis or by the decompilation when the values of memory locations are lost. As mentioned, even if we do not produce the gas formula, we know that the gas consumption is *finite* (otherwise the system flags a ranking function error described below). (ii) *Ranking function error:* The solver needs to find ranking functions to bound the maximum number of iterations of all loops the analyzed code might perform. If GASTAP fails at this step, it outputs a *ranking function error*. Sect. 3 has described a scenario where we have stumbled across this kind of error. We note that number of these failures for **mem** is lower than for **opcode** because when the cost accumulated in a loop is 0, PUBS does not look for a ranking function. (iii) *Cover point error:* The equations are transformed into direct recursive form to be solved [5]. If the transformation is not feasible, a *cover point error* is thrown. This might happen when we have mutually recursive functions, but it also happens for nested loops as in non-structured languages. This is because they contain jump instructions from the inner loop to the outer, and vice versa, and become mutually recursive. A loop extraction transformation would solve this problem, and we leave its implementation for the future work.

Table 3. Timing breakdown for GASTAP on the analyzed 29,061 smart contracts

Phase	T_{opcode} (s)	T_{mem} (s)	T_{total} (s)	%opc	%mem	%total
CFG generation (OYENTE*)	—	—	17,075.55	—	—	1.384%
RBR generation (ETHIR*)	—	—	81.37	—	—	0.006%
Size analysis (SACO)	—	—	105,732	—	—	8.57%
Generation of gas equations	141,576	125,760	267,336	11.48%	10.2%	21.68%
Solving gas equation (PUBS)	395,429	447,502	842,931	32.06%	36.3%	68.36%
Total time GASTAP			1,233,155.92			100%

As regards the efficiency of GASTAP, the total analysis time for all functions is 1,233,155.92 s (342.54 h). Columns **T** and **%** show, resp., the time in seconds for each phase and the percentage of the total for each type of gas bound. The first three rows are common for the inference of the opcode and memory bounds, while equation generation and solving is separated for opcode and memory. Most of the time is spent in solving the GE (68.36%), which includes some timeouts. The time taken by ETHIR is negligible, as it is a syntactic transformation process, while all other parts require semantic reasoning. All in all, we argue that the statistics from our experimental evaluation show the accuracy, effectiveness and efficiency of our tool. Also, the sources of incompleteness point out directions for further improvements of the tool.

4   Related Work and Conclusions

Analysis of Ethereum smart contracts for possible safety violations and security and vulnerabilities is a popular topic that has received a lot of attention recently, with numerous tools developed, leveraging techniques based on symbolic execution [19,20,22,23,25,27], SMT solving [21,24], and certified programming [7,9,18], with only a small fraction of them focusing on analyzing gas consumption.

The GASPER tool identifies gas-costly programming patterns [11], which can be optimized to consume less. For doing so, it relies on matching specific control-flow patterns, SMT solvers and symbolic computation, which makes their analysis neither sound, nor complete. In a similar vein, the recent work by Grech *et al.* [17] identifies a number of classes of gas-focused vulnerabilities, and provides MADMAX, a static analysis, also working on a decompiled EVM bytecode, data-combining techniques from flow analysis together with CFA context-sensitive analysis and modeling of memory layout. In its techniques, MADMAX differs from GASTAP, as it focuses on identifying control- and data-flow patterns inherent for the gas-related vulnerabilities, thus, working as a bug-finder, rather than complexity analyzer. Since deriving accurate worst-case complexity boundaries is not a goal of any of both GASPER and MADMAX, they are unsuitable for tackling the challenge 1, which we have posed in the introduction.

In a concurrent work, Marescotti *et al.* identified three cases in which computing gas consumption can help in making Ethereum more efficient: (a) prevent errors causing contracts get stuck with *out-of-gas* exception, (b) place the right price on the gas unit, and (c) recognize semantically-equivalent smart contracts [24]. They propose a methodology, based on the notion of the so-called *gas consumption paths* (GCPs) to estimate the worst-case gas consumption using techniques from symbolic bounded model checking [10]. Their approach is based on symbolically enumerating all execution paths and unwinding loops to a limit. Instead, using resource analysis, GASTAP infers the maximal number of iterations for loops and generates accurate gas bounds which are valid for any possible execution of the function and not only for the unwound paths. Besides, the approach by Marescotti *et al.* has not been implemented in the context of EVM and has not been evaluated on real-world smart contracts as ours.

Conclusions. Automated static reasoning about resource consumption is critical for developing safe and secure blockchain-based replicated computations, managing billions of dollars worth of virtual currency. In this work, we employed state-of-the art techniques in resource analysis, showing that such reasoning is feasible for Ethereum, where it can be used at scale not only for detecting vulnerabilities, but also for verification/certification of existing smart contracts.

References

1. The **EthereumPot** contract (2017). https://etherscan.io/address/0x5a13caa 82851342e14cd2ad0257707cddb8a31b7
2. Etherscan (2018). https://etherscan.io
3. Oyente: An Analysis Tool for Smart Contracts (2018). https://github.com/melonproject/oyente

4. Albert, E., et al.: SACO: static analyzer for concurrent objects. In: Ábrahám, E., Havelund, K. (eds.) TACAS 2014. LNCS, vol. 8413, pp. 562–567. Springer, Heidelberg (2014). https://doi.org/10.1007/978-3-642-54862-8_46

5. Albert, E., Arenas, P., Genaim, S., Puebla, G.: Automatic inference of upper bounds for recurrence relations in cost analysis. In: Alpuente, M., Vidal, G. (eds.) SAS 2008. LNCS, vol. 5079, pp. 221–237. Springer, Heidelberg (2008). https://doi.org/10.1007/978-3-540-69166-2_15

6. Albert, E., Gordillo, P., Livshits, B., Rubio, A., Sergey, I.: ETHIR: a framework for high-level analysis of ethereum bytecode. In: Lahiri, S.K., Wang, C. (eds.) ATVA 2018. LNCS, vol. 11138, pp. 513–520. Springer, Cham (2018). https://doi.org/10.1007/978-3-030-01090-4_30

7. Amani, S., Bégel, M., Bortin, M., Staples, M.: Towards verifying ethereum smart contract bytecode in Isabelle/HOL. In: CPP 2018, pp. 66–77. ACM (2018)

8. Bernani, T.: Oraclize (2016). http://www.oraclize.it

9. Bhargavan, K., et al.: Formal verification of smart contracts: short paper. In: PLAS 2016, pp. 91–96. ACM (2016)

10. Biere, A., Cimatti, A., Clarke, E., Zhu, Y.: Symbolic model checking without BDDs. In: Cleaveland, W.R. (ed.) TACAS 1999. LNCS, vol. 1579, pp. 193–207. Springer, Heidelberg (1999). https://doi.org/10.1007/3-540-49059-0_14

11. Chen, T., Li, X., Luo, X., Zhang, X.: Under-optimized smart contracts devour your money. In: SANER 2017, pp. 442–446. IEEE Computer Society (2017)

12. Cousot, P., Halbwachs, N.: Automatic discovery of linear restraints among variables of aprogram. In: POPL 1978, pp. 84–96 (1978)

13. Ethereum. Solidity (2018). https://solidity.readthedocs.io

14. Ethereum. Vyper (2018). https://vyper.readthedocs.io

15. Flores-Montoya, A., Hähnle, R.: Resource analysis of complex programs with cost equations. In: Garrigue, J. (ed.) APLAS 2014. LNCS, vol. 8858, pp. 275–295. Springer, Cham (2014). https://doi.org/10.1007/978-3-319-12736-1_15

16. Ethereum Foundation. Safety - Ethereum Wiki (2018). https://github.com/ethereum/wiki/wiki/Safety. Accessed on 14 Nov 2018

17. Grech, N., Kong, M., Jurisevic, A., Brent, L., Scholz, B., Smaragdakis, Y.: Madmax: surviving out-of-gas conditions in ethereum smart contracts. In: PACMPL, 2(OOPSLA), pp. 116:1–116:27 (2018)

18. Grishchenko, I., Maffei, M., Schneidewind, C.: A semantic framework for the security analysis of ethereum smart contracts. In: Bauer, L., Küsters, R. (eds.) POST 2018. LNCS, vol. 10804, pp. 243–269. Springer, Cham (2018). https://doi.org/10.1007/978-3-319-89722-6_10

19. Grossman, S., et al.: Online detection of effectively callback free objects with applications to smart contracts. In: PACMPL, 2(POPL), pp. 48:1–48:28 (2018)

20. Kalra, S., Goel, S., Dhawan, M., Sharma, S.: ZEUS: analyzing safety of smart contracts. In: NDSS 2018. The Internet Society (2018)

21. Kolluri, A., Nikolic, I., Sergey, I., Hobor, A., Saxena, P.: Exploiting The Laws of Order in Smart Contracts. CoRR, abs/1810.11605 (2018)

22. Krupp, J., Rossow, C.: Teether: Gnawing at ethereum to automatically exploit smart contracts. In: USENIX Security Symposium, pp. 1317–1333. USENIX Association (2018)

23. Luu, L., Chu, D., Olickel, H., Saxena, P., Hobor, A.: Making smart contracts smarter. In CCS 2016, pp. 254–269. ACM (2016)

24. Marescotti, M., Blicha, M., Hyvärinen, A.E.J., Asadi, S., Sharygina, N.: Computing exact worst-case gas consumption for smart contracts. In: Margaria, T., Steffen, B. (eds.) ISoLA 2018. LNCS, vol. 11247, pp. 450–465. Springer, Cham (2018). https://doi.org/10.1007/978-3-030-03427-6_33
25. Nikolic, I., Kolluri, A., Sergey, I., Saxena, P., Hobor, A.: Finding the greedy, prodigal, and suicidal contracts at scale. In: ACSAC 2018, pp. 653–663. ACM (2018)
26. Suiche, M.: Porosity: A Decompiler For Blockchain-Based Smart Contracts Bytecode (2017)
27. Tsankov, P., Dan, A.M., Drachsler-Cohen, D., Gervais, A., Bünzli, F., Vechev, M.T.: Securify: practical security analysis of smart contracts. In: CCS 2018, pp. 67–82. ACM (2018)
28. Wegbreit, B.: Mechanical program analysis. Commun. ACM **18**(9), 528–539 (1975)
29. Wood, G.: Ethereum: A secure decentralised generalised transaction ledger (2014)

Estimating Latency for Synchronous Dataflow Graphs Using Periodic Schedules

Philippe Glanon$^{(\boxtimes)}$, Selma Azaiez, and Chokri Mraidha

CEA-LIST Saclay, Gif-sur-yvette, France
{philippe.glanon,selma.azaiez,chokri.mraidha}@cea.fr

Abstract. Synchronous Dataflow Graph (SDFG) is a formal tool widely used to model and analyze the behaviour of systems constrained by timing requirements. It has been successfully used in digital signal processing and manufacturing fields to specify and analyze the performance of embedded and distributed applications. Various performance indicators such as throughput, latency or memory consumption can be evaluated with SDFGs. This paper tackles the latency analysis for SDFG using periodic schedules.

Keywords: Synchronous dataflow · Latency · Periodic schedules

1 Introduction

SDFG is a formal model initially introduced in [11] to describe communications in digital signal processing applications of which performance is usually important. In the Petri net community, the SDFG is known as Weighted Event Graph (WEG) [9] and is often used to model the behaviour of automated production systems [5]. In this paper, we adopt the notation SDFG instead of WEG. Describing an application using to the SDFG aims to foster its performance analysis by means of algorithms with good mathematical foundations. Although throughput is a very interesting performance indicator for applications, latency is another important performance metric that can be analyzed to deploy a valid and implementable application at design-time. Latency is generally defined as the time gap between the moment that a stimulation appears in a system and the moment that its reaction begins or ends. Analyzing latency for an application implies to compute and optimize delays in its specification model so that tasks could be executed with reasonable delays. To the best of our knowledge, latency is so far the performance metric very little studied for application modeled with SDFGs compared to other performance indicators such as throughput and resource consumption.

In [3], latency has been studied for a particular class of SDFG called real-time SDFGs (RTSDFGs). A RTSDFG is a SDFG to model exclusively real-time applications where timing constraints such as release dates and periods are

© Crown 2019
P. Ganty and M. Kaâniche (Eds.): VECoS 2019, LNCS 11847, pp. 79–94, 2019.
https://doi.org/10.1007/978-3-030-35092-5_6

assumed to be known. Therefore, for applications where these constraints are not specified, analysis techniques developed in [3] can not be used to estimate latency metrics.

In [6], latency has only been studied for a subclass of SDFG noted as homogeneous SDFG (HSDFG) [11]. In theory, it is possible to compute the latency reachable by a SDFG, by first converting it into an equivalent HSDFG [1] and then scheduling the HSDFG to determine the optimal latency metrics. However, converting a SDFG into an HSDFG can lead to an exponential size graph (in terms of number of nodes) than the original graph and can increase the worst-case complexity of scheduling algorithms for HSDFG. Therefore, to analyze the latency of SDFGs it is more preferable to develop techniques working directly on SDFG topologies instead of HSDFG structures.

A latency computation approach has been proposed in [8] that provides the optimal latency reachable by a SDFG under a throughput constraint. This approach works directly on SDFG topologies and is based on self-time schedules. Indeed, the self-time schedule [6] for a SDFG is an as soon as possible (ASAP) scheduling policy that consists in firing nodes of a graph as soon as the necessary data is available. Such a schedule exhibits two phases, a transient phase followed by a steady phase where firings of actors have a cyclic behaviour. However, depending on the topology of the SDFG, the number of firings required for the transient phase can be bounded by a non-polynomial function. This can make complex the analysis of the SDFG.

In this paper, we propose an alternative analysis approach to compute latency for SDFG structures. Our analysis approach is based on periodic schedules [2,5]. Indeed, periodic schedules are alternative strategies to analyze the timing behaviour of a SDFG. Although such scheduling policies may be dominated by ASAP schedules, there polynomial time-complexity makes them very useful to analyze SDFGs. Detailed comparison of polynomial and ASAP schedules for SDFGs are provided in [5].

The latency analysis approach proposed in this paper mainly consists of two steps. In the first step, we transform a SDFG into a normalized graph using the technique developed in [7] and then according to the definition of periodic schedules we characterize and compute the optimal (i.e. maximal or minimal) latency reachable by the normalized graph. This latency is called optimal periodic latency in this paper.

The rest of the paper is structured as follows. In the Sect. 2, we provide a formal definition of the SDFG and we illustrate its modeling power through a running example. In the Sect. 3, we characterize feasible periodic schedules for SDFGs. In the Sect. 4, we characterize and compute the optimal periodic latency for SDFG. In the Sect. 5, we evaluate the time-complexity of our approach by running it on several instances of SDFGs and we draw some conclusions in Sect. 6.

2   Synchronous Dataflow Graph

2.1   A Formal Definition of SDFG

A SDFG is a directed graph G_{sdf} where nodes (called actors) represent computations and arcs (called channels) are FIFO channels representing communications between actors. Actors can communicate via channels by exchanging tokens. Formally, a SDFG can be defined as a tuple $G_{sdf} = (\mathcal{A}, E, \mathcal{P}, \mathcal{C}, M_0, \mathcal{L})$ where:

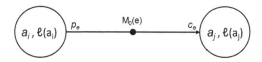

Fig. 1. A graphical representation of a SDFG where $\mathcal{A} = \{a_i, a_j\}$, $E = \{e\}$, $P = \{p_e\}$, $P = \{p_e\}$, $M_0 = M_0(e)$ and $\mathcal{L} = \{\ell(a_i), \ell(a_j)\}$.

- $\mathcal{A}$ is the set of actors.
- E is the set of channels.
- $\mathcal{P} = \{p(e)|e \in E\}$ is the set of production rates determined by the function $p : E \rightarrow \mathbb{N}*$ which associates to each channel $e \in E$ a production rate $p(e) = p_e$.
- $\mathcal{C} = \{c(e)|e \in E\}$ is the set of consumption rates in the graph. It is determined by the function $c : E \rightarrow \mathbb{N}*$ which associates to each channel $e \in E$ a consumption rate $c(e) = c_e$.
- $M_0 = \{M(0)(e)|e \in E\}$ is the initial marking of the graph. It is determined by the function $M : E \rightarrow \mathbb{N}$ which associates to each channel $e \in E$ a non-negative integer $M_0(e)$.
- $\mathcal{L} = \{\ell(t_i)(a)|a \in \mathcal{A}\}$ is the set of values taken by the function $\ell : \mathcal{A} \rightarrow \mathbb{N}$ which associates to each actor $a \in \mathcal{A}$ an execution time $\ell(a)$.

Figure 1 shows a graphical representation of a SDFG. For the rest of the paper, a channel $e \in E$ will be characterized by the tuple $(a_i, a_j, p_e, c_e, M_0(e))$ where $a_i, a_j \in \mathcal{A}$ are respectively producer and consumer actors associated with the channel. Values $p_e \in \mathcal{P}$ and $c_e \in \mathcal{C}$ are respectively its production and consumption rates while $M_0(e)$ represents its initial marking.

2.2   Running Example

Let us consider an automated production system consisting of a sensor C_s, a production machine C_m, two loading robots C_{r1}, C_{r2} and one unloading robot C_{r3}, all involved in the production of a finished product P. In order to produce P, two types of raw material M_1 and M_2 are required. The production of a single unit of P follows steps below:

- **Sensing step:** a sensor C_s sends a starting signal sampled into bytes of starting data to loading robots C_{r1} and C_{r2}.

– **Loading step:** when robots C_{r1} and C_{r2} receive bytes of starting data coming from C_s, they respectively load a single part of M_1 and M_2 onto C_m. More precisely, C_{r1} requires two bytes of starting data to load one part of M_1 onto the machine C_m. Conversely, to load one part of M_2 on C_m, the robot C_{r2} requires three bytes of starting data. When a robot loads one part of raw material on C_m, it simultaneously sends one byte of information data to C_m.

Table 1. Duration of production tasks for the modeling example

Tasks	sensing	loading M_1	loading M_2	Producing P	unloading P
Components	C_s	C_{r1}	C_{r2}	C_m	C_{r3}
Durations	2	4	3	6	3
Actors	a_1	a_2	a_3	a_4	a_5

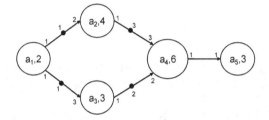

Fig. 2. SDFG corresponding to the running example.

– **Machining step:** to produce a single unit of P, the machine C_m uses two parts of M_1 and three parts of M_2. Therefore, C_m requires respectively two and three bytes of information data coming from C_{r1} and C_{r2} before producing a single unit of P.
– **Unloading step:** when C_m produces one unit of P, it sends one byte of unloading data to the robot C_{r3} which unloads the product P from C_m.

At the beginning of the production process, it is assumed that one byte of starting data is available both to robots C_{r1} and C_{r2}. It is also assumed that two parts of M_1 and three parts of M_2 were available onto the machine C_m. Table 1 shows the duration of tasks executed by each component of the production system (i.e. the sensor, robots and assembling machine). In this table, we also describe SDFG actors corresponding to tasks executed by components and we depict in Fig. 2 the full SDFG that models the production system. In this SDFG, actors represent tasks executed by system components and channels model exchanges of data between actors.

Note that this SDFG does not contain cycles which means that it is not strongly connected. Indeed, in this paper, we limit our latency analysis study only to connected SDFGs. Even if our analysis approach can be extended to evaluate the optimal periodic latency in strongly connected SDFGs we do not tackle such a problem in this paper.

3   Periodic Schedules and Precedences Relations

In order to analyze the performance of SDFG-based applications at design-time, static scheduling strategies are used to execute the SDFG actors. All these scheduling strategies can be classified into ASAP and periodic schedules [2]. In an ASAP schedule, actors are executed as soon as their data are available while in a periodic schedule, they are executed following regular time intervals denoted by periods. In this paper, we are only interested by periodic schedules. However, before scheduling a SDFG, we need to define its schedulability conditions as well as precedences constraints between its actors.

3.1   Schedulability Conditions

Consistency and liveness are necessary and sufficient conditions that determine the schedulability of a SDFG. When a SDFG is consistent and live it is proved in [11] that there exists a periodic admissible sequential (or parallel) schedule where actors can be executed infinitely often.

Definition 1 (Consistency and repetition vector). *Let consider a SDFG $G_{sdf} = (\mathcal{A}, E, \mathcal{P}, \mathcal{C}, M_0, \mathcal{L})$. G_{sdf} is consistent if there exists a function $n : E \to \mathbb{N}*$ which associates to each actor, a strictly positive integer such that for any channel $e = (a_i, a_j, p_e, c_e, M_0(e)) \in E$, $p_e.n(a_i) = c_e.n(a_j)$. The set of values provided by such function determines the repetition vector $N = [n(a_1), ..., n(a_{|A|})]$ associated with G_{sdf}.*

For a consistent SDFG, components of the repetition vector are called repetition factors and they indicate for each actor the minimum number of executions required in a periodic admissible schedule so that the graph could iterate again (i.e it could reach its initial marking again). The SDFG given in Fig. 2 is consistent and its repetition vector is $N = [6, 3, 2, 1, 1]$.

Definition 2 (Liveness). *Let $G_{sdf} = (\mathcal{A}, E, \mathcal{P}, \mathcal{C}, M_0, \mathcal{L})$ be a SDFG. G_{sdf} is live if its initial marking enables to execute actors infinitely often.*

A live SDFG is a graph where actors can be executed without deadlocks. The liveliness checking problem for SDFG is a NP-hard problem widely addressed in the dataflow community. Various analysis algorithms have been proposed in [7,8] to check the liveness of SDFG. The SDFG given in Fig. 2 is also live because its initial marking enables to execute infinitely often its actors.

For the rest of this paper, we assume that only consistent and live SDFGs are used to estimate the optimal periodic latency.

3.2   Execution Instances and Precedence Relations

In any SDFG, actors can be executed as many times as possible according to the repetition vector. Therefore, to schedule a SDFG, it is important to characterize execution instances of actors as well as precedence relations between these instances.

Definition 3 (Execution Instance). *Let $G_{sdf} = (\mathcal{A}, E, \mathcal{P}, \mathcal{C}, M_0, \mathcal{L})$ be a SDFG and n_i be a strictly positive integer. For any actor $a_i \in \mathcal{A}$, $\langle a_i, n_i \rangle$ represents its nth execution instance.*

Definition 4 (Precedence Relation). *Let $G_{sdf} = (\mathcal{A}, E, \mathcal{P}, \mathcal{C}, M_0, \mathcal{L})$ be a SDFG and (n_i, n_j) be a couple of strictly positive integers. A channel $e = (a_i, a_j, p_e, c_e, M_0(e)) \in E$ induces a precedence relation from $\langle a_i, n_i \rangle$ to $\langle a_j, n_j \rangle$ if and only if following conditions hold:*

- **Condition 1:** *$\langle a_j, n_j \rangle$ can be executed after $\langle a_i, n_i \rangle$*
- **Condition 2:** *$\langle a_j, n_j - 1 \rangle$ can be executed before $\langle a_i, n_i \rangle$ but $\langle a_j, n_j \rangle$ cannot.*

For any schedule S, such a precedence relation induces the following inequality where $S(a_i, n_i)$ and $S(a_j, n_j)$ are respectively the starting time of actors a_i and a_j in the schedule S:

$$S(a_i, n_i) + \ell(a_i) \leq S(a_j, n_j). \tag{1}$$

The set of precedences relations induced by any SDFG channel is formally characterized by the Lemma 1 which was proved in [7].

Lemma 1. *Let us consider a SDFG $G_{sdf} = (\mathcal{A}, E, \mathcal{P}, \mathcal{C}, M_0, \mathcal{L})$. Let (n_i, n_j) be a couple of strictly positive integers. For any channel $e = (a_i, a_j, p_e, c_e, M_0(e)) \in E$, a precedence relation is induced from $\langle a_i, n_i \rangle$ to $\langle a_j, n_j \rangle$ if and only if:*

$$p_e > M_0(e) + p_e \cdot n_i - c_e \cdot n_j \geq max\{p_e - c_e, 0\}. \tag{2}$$

For a given SDFG, precedences relations induced between all execution instances of actors can be checked by applying Lemma 1. E.g. in the SDFG depicted in Fig. 2, we can prove that a channel $e = (a_2, a_4, 1, 3, 3)$ induces a precedence relation from $\langle a_2, 3 \rangle$ to $\langle a_4, 2 \rangle$ as follows:

$$1 > 3 + 1 \cdot 3 - 3 \cdot 2 \geq max\{1 - 3, 0\}$$

Lemma 2 was introduced and proved in [5] as a corollary of the Lemma 1 to characterize couples of strictly positive integers (n_i, n_j) for which a precedence relation exists from $\langle a_i, n_i \rangle$ to $\langle a_j, n_j \rangle$.

Lemma 2. *Let $e = (a_i, a_j, p_e, c_e, M_0(e))$ be a channel of a SDFG G_{sdf} and let us consider integer values $k_{min} = \frac{max\{p_e - c_e, 0\} - M_0(e)}{gcd_e}$ and $k_{max} = \frac{p_e - M_0(e)}{gcd_e} - 1$ where $gcd_e = gcd(p_e, c_e)$. For any integer $k \in \{k_{min}, ..., k_{max}\}$, there exists an infinite tuple $(n_i, n_j) \in (\mathbb{N}^*)^2$ such that $p_e.n_i - c_e \cdot n_j = k \cdot gcd_e$ and the channel e induces a precedence relation from $\langle a_i, n_i \rangle$ to $\langle a_j, n_j \rangle$.*

3.3 Periodic Schedules for SDFG

According to [2] and [5], periodic schedules for any SDFG are defined as follows:

Definition 5 (Periodic Schedules). *Let* $G_{sdf} = (\mathcal{A}, E, \mathcal{P}, \mathcal{C}, M_0, \mathcal{L})$ *be a SDFG. A schedule of* G_{sdf} *is a function* $S : A \to \mathbb{N}^*$ *which associates a starting time* $S(a_i, n_i)$ *to any execution instance* $\langle a_i, n_i \rangle$ *of any actor* $a_i \in \mathcal{A}$*. If* S *is periodic then, for any actor* $a_i \in A$*, there exists an execution period* $w_i \geq \ell(a_i)$ *such that:*

- $S(a_i, 1) \geq 0$.
- $S(a_i, n_i) = S(a_i, 1) + (n_i - 1) \cdot w_i, \forall \langle a_i, n_i \rangle$.

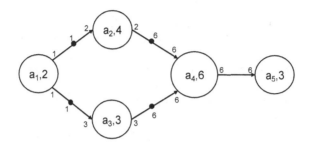

Fig. 3. Normalized graph equivalent to the SDFG depicted in Fig. 2.

For any SDFG, a periodic schedule S is feasible if it satisfies precedences relations induced by its channels (see Subsect. 3.2). Moreover, according to [5], S is optimal if it provides a minimal execution period for each actor in the SDFG.

In order to compute the optimal periodic latency for a SDFG, we first need to characterize precedence relations according to optimal feasible periodic schedules. These constraints are characterized in the following section.

4   Latency Analysis Approach

In this section, we present our latency analysis approach for SDFGs. We describe our approach over three subsections. In the first subsection, we define the normalization [7] and we present the main property of normalized SDFGs. In the second subsection, we characterize and compute the optimal periodic latency induced by a channel belonging to a normalized SDFG and in the last subsection, we characterize and compute the optimal periodic latency reachable by the normalized graph.

4.1   Normalization of SDFG

Normalization is a polynomial transformation introduced in [7] to transform a SDFG into its equivalent graph called normalized SDFG. Such transformation is often applied to reduce the analysis complexity of SDFGs. In [2] and [5] it has been applied to compute the optimal periodic throughput for SDFGs. A SDFG $G_{sdf} = (\mathcal{A}, E, \mathcal{P}, \mathcal{C}, M_0, \mathcal{L})$ is called normalized if for any actor $a_i \in \mathcal{A}$, production and consumption rates of a_i are equals.

Definition 6 (Normalization). *Let $G_{sdf} = (\mathcal{A}, E, \mathcal{P}, \mathcal{C}, M_0, \mathcal{L})$ be a SDFG. G_{sdf} is normalizable if there exists a function $z : A \rightarrow \mathbb{N}^*$ which associates to each actor a strictly positive integer such that for any channel $e = (a_i, a_j, p_e, c_e, M_0(e)) \in E$, $\frac{z(a_i)}{p_e} = \frac{z(a_j)}{c_e}$ with $z(a_i) = z_i$ and $z(a_j) = z_j$. The set of values provided by the function z determines the normalization vector $Z = [z_1, ..., z_{|A|}] = [z(a_1), ..., z(a_{|A|})]$ associated with G_{sdf}. Components of a normalization vector are called normalization factors and they characterize both production and consumption rates of the actors in the equivalent normalized SDFG of G_{sdf}.*

More details on normalization are provided in [5] and [7]. The normalized graph equivalent to the SDFG showed in Fig. 2 is depicted in Fig. 3 where the normalization vector $Z = [1, 2, 3, 6, 6]$. Note that the marking of channels in a normalized graph is calculated according to normalization factors as well as the marking of channels belonging to the original graph.

In order to characterize feasible periodic schedules for normalized SDFGs. Theorem 1 was introduced and proved in [5].

Theorem 1. *Let $G_{sdf} = (\mathcal{A}, E, \mathcal{P}, \mathcal{C}, M_0, \mathcal{L})$ be a normalized SDFG and $Z = [z_1, ..., z_{|A|}]$ be its normalization vector. For any feasible periodic schedule S, there exists a strictly positive rational K called average token flow time such that for any actor $a_i \in A$, $\frac{w_i}{z_i} = K$ where w_i is the period of actor a_i. Moreover, precedences relations associated with any channel $e \in E$ are fulfilled by S if and only if:*

$$S(a_j, 1) - S(a_i, 1) \geq \ell(a_i) + K \cdot (z_j - M_0(e) - gcd_e). \tag{3}$$

4.2   Optimal Periodic Latency Induced by a Channel

In order to calculate the optimal periodic latency for a SDFG, we first need to characterize and compute the optimal periodic latency induced by its channel. In this subsection, we characterize and calculate minimal and maximal periodic latencies induced by any channel belonging to a normalized SDFG.

Before computing such latency metrics, we provide the following definition to characterize the latency between two dependent execution instances.

Definition 7 (Latency between execution instances). *Let $G_{sdf} = (\mathcal{A}, E, \mathcal{P}, \mathcal{C}, M_0, \mathcal{L})$ be a SDFG and let S be a feasible schedule of G_{sdf}. For any couple of strictly positive integers (n_i, n_j), if a channel $e = (a_i, a_j, p_e, c_e, M_0(e)) \in E$ induces a precedence relation from $\langle a_i, n_i \rangle$ to $\langle a_j, n_j \rangle$ then, the latency induced by the channel e is defined as the time elapsed between the beginning $\langle a_i, n_i \rangle$ and the end of $\langle a_j, n_j \rangle$. More formally, such latency is expressed as follows:*

$$Lat_{\{n_i, n_j\}}(a_i, a_j) = (S(a_j, n_j) + \ell(a_j)) - S(a_i, n_i). \tag{4}$$

Note that Definition 7 can be applied both for the normalized and non-normalized SDFG. By this definition, we propose the following lemma to characterize the optimal periodic latency induced by a channel belonging to a normalized SDFG.

Lemma 3. *Let consider a normalized SDFG $G_{sdf} = (\mathcal{A}, E, \mathcal{P}, \mathcal{C}, M_0, \mathcal{L})$ and $Z = [z_1, ..., z_{|A|}]$ be its normalization vector. Let $e = (a_i, a_j, p_e, c_e, M_0(e)) \in E$ be a channel of G_{sdf} and (n_i, n_j) be a couple of strictly positive integers. In a feasible periodic schedule S, let w_i and w_j be respectively periods associated with actors a_i and a_j. In the schedule S, if $\langle a_i, n_i \rangle$ precedes $\langle a_j, n_j \rangle$ then, the latency induced by the channel e is equal to:*

$$Lat_{\{n_i, n_j\}}(a_i, a_j) = S(a_j, 1) - S(a_i, 1) - \frac{w_i}{p_e} \cdot k \cdot gcd_e + w_i - w_j + \ell(a_j). \quad (5)$$

Proof. Let assume that the channel $e = (a_i, a_j, p_e, c_e, M_0(e)) \in E$ induces a precedence relation from $\langle a_i, n_i \rangle$ to $\langle a_i, n_i \rangle$. As S is a feasible periodic schedule, according to Eq. 4 and Definition 5, the latency between $\langle a_i, n_i \rangle$ and $\langle a_i, n_i \rangle$ is given by the following equation where $w_i \geq 0$ and $w_j \geq 0$ are periods respectively associated with actors a_i and a_j in the schedule S:

$$Lat_{\{n_i, n_j\}}(a_i, a_j) = (S(a_j, 1) + (n_j - 1) \cdot w_j + \ell(a_j)) - S(a_i, 1) - (n_i - 1) \cdot w_i.$$

By developing and ordering this equation, we get:

$$Lat_{\{n_i, n_j\}}(a_i, a_j) = S(a_j, 1) - S(a_i, 1) + n_j \cdot w_j - n_i \cdot w_i + w_i - w_j + \ell(a_j).$$

As G_{sdf} is normalized, by Theorem 1, we get $\frac{w_i}{z_i} = \frac{w_j}{z_j} = K$. This implies:

$$Lat_{\{n_i, n_j\}}(a_i, a_j) = S(a_j, 1) - S(a_i, 1) + \frac{w_i}{z_i} \cdot (n_j \cdot z_j - n_i \cdot z_i) + w_i - w_j + \ell(a_j).$$

By Definition 6, the normalization factor z_i (resp. z_j) represents both production and consumption rates of the actor a_i (resp. a_j). Therefore, for the channel e, $p_e = z_i$ and $c_e = z_j$ and we get:

$$Lat_{\{n_i, n_j\}}(a_i, a_j) = S(a_j, 1) - S(a_i, 1) + \frac{w_i}{p_e} \cdot (n_j \cdot c_e - n_i \cdot p_e) + w_i - w_j + \ell(a_j).$$

Finally, by Lemma 2, there exists $k \in \{k_{min}, ..., k_{max}\}$ such that $p_e \cdot n_i - c_e \cdot n_j = k.gcd_e$. Therefore:

$$Lat_{\{n_i, n_j\}}(a_i, a_j) = S(a_j, 1) - S(a_i, 1) - \frac{w_i}{p_e} \cdot k \cdot gcd_e + w_i - w_j + \ell(a_j). \quad \square$$

In order to calculate the optimal periodic latency reachable by a normalized SDFG, we first need to characterize the optimal periodic latency induced by its channel. By using Lemma 3, we can now characterize minimal and maximal periodic latencies induced by any channel belonging to a normalized SDFG. This characterization is provided by the following theorem.

Theorem 2. *Let consider a normalized SDFG $G_{sdf} = (\mathcal{A}, E, \mathcal{P}, \mathcal{C}, M_0, \mathcal{L})$. Let $e = (a_i, a_j, p_e, c_e, M_0(e)) \in E$ be a channel of G_{sdf}. In a feasible periodic schedule*

S of G_{sdf}, minimum and maximum periodic latencies induced by the channel e between actors a_i and a_j are defined as follows:

$$Lat_{min}(a_i, a_j) = S(a_j, 1) - S(a_i, 1) + \frac{w_i}{p_e} \cdot (M_0(e) - p_e + gcd_e) + w_i - w_j + \ell(a_j).$$
(6)

$$Lat_{max}(a_i, a_j) = S(a_j, 1) - S(a_i, 1) + \frac{w_i}{p_e} \cdot (M_0(e) - max\{p_e - c_e, 0\}) + w_i - w_j + \ell(a_j). \quad (7)$$

Proof. For any couple of strictly positive integers (n_i, n_j), let assume that the channel e induces a precedence relation from $\langle a_i, n_i \rangle$ to $\langle a_i, n_i \rangle$. By Lemma 3:

$$Lat_{\{n_i, n_j\}}(a_i, a_j) = S(a_j, 1) - S(a_i, 1) - \frac{w_i}{p_e} \cdot k \cdot gcd_e + w_i - w_j + \ell(a_j).$$

According to Lemma 2, $k \in \{k_{min}, ..., k_{max}\}$. Thus, by replacing k by its maximum value k_{max}, we get the minimal periodic latency induced by the channel e:

$$Lat_{min}(a_i, a_j) = S(a_j, 1) - S(a_i, 1) + \frac{w_i}{p_e} \cdot (M_0(e) - p_e + gcd_e) + w_i - w_j + \ell(a_j).$$

Conversely, if we replace k by its minimum value k_{min}, we obtain the characterization of the maximum periodic latency induced by the channel e between actors a_i and a_j. This latency is expressed as follows:

$$Lat_{max}(a_i, a_j) = S(a_j, 1) - S(a_i, 1) + \frac{w_i}{p_e} \cdot (M_0(e) - max\{p_e - c_e, 0\}) + w_i - w_j + \ell(a_j).$$
$\square$

According to Theorem 2, we can compute minimal/maximal periodic latency metrics for any channel $e = (a_i, a_j, p_e, c_e, M_0(e))$ belonging to a normalized graph $G_{sdf} = (\mathcal{A}, E, \mathcal{P}, \mathcal{C}, M_0, \mathcal{L})$ by applying respectively Eqs. 6 and 7. However, before computing these metrics, we need to determine the optimal feasible periodic schedule that gives starting times and optimal execution periods for actors belonging to G_{sdf}. To achieve this, we formulate and solve the linear program (P):

$$(P) \begin{cases} obj = minimize(w_i) \\ S(a_j, 1) - S(a_i, 1) \geq \dfrac{w_i}{p_e} \cdot (c_e - M_0(e) - gcd_e) + \ell(a_i), \ \forall \ e \ \in E. \ (1) \\ S(a_i, 1) \geq 0, \ \forall \ a_i \ \in \mathcal{A}. \hspace{4cm} (2) \end{cases}$$

In the linear program (P), the constraint (1) establishes precedences relations for any channel in G_{sdf}. This constraint is derived from Theorem 1 and Definition 6. For any actor $a_i \in A$, the constraint (2) expresses that the starting time of its first execution instance is a positive value. The objective function (obj) of this linear program is to minimize periods of all actors belonging to G_{sdf}.

For any normalized SDFG, the solution of this linear program is an optimal feasible periodic schedule S that provides for each actor, the optimal period as well as the starting time of the first execution instance. These parameters are then replaced in Eqs. 6 and 7 to compute respectively the minimal and maximal periodic latency induced by any channel.

For the normalized graph depicted in Fig. 3, an optimal feasible periodic schedule S is depicted in Fig. 4. According to this schedule, the latency computation parameters can be extract and replaced in Eqs. 6 and 7 to calculate either the minimal/maximal periodic latency induced by channels. For example, let consider the channel $e = (a_2, a_4, 2, 6, 6)$ in the normalized graph, the minimal and maximal periodic latency induced by the channel e are respectively given by:

$$Lat_{min}(a_2, a_4) = 0 - 2 + \frac{6}{2} \cdot (6 - 2 + 2) + 6 - 18 + 6 = 10.$$

$$Lat_{max}(a_2, a_4) = 0 - 2 + \frac{6}{2} \cdot (6 - max\{2 - 6, 0\}) + 6 - 18 + 6 = 10.$$

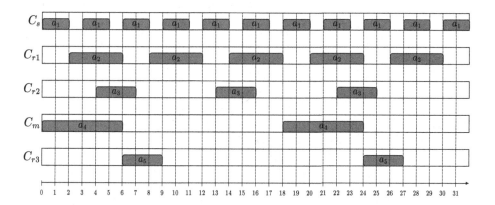

Fig. 4. An optimal feasible periodic schedule of normalized graph depicted in Fig. 2.

Note that minimal and maximal periodic latency values induced by the channel $e = (a_2, a_4, 1, 3, 3)$ are equal to each other because of the initial marking of the graph as well as production and consumption rates of attached actors. In some case, these latency metrics may not be equal.

4.3   Optimal Periodic Latency Reachable by a Normalized SDFG

In the previous subsection, we characterized the minimum and maximum periodic latency induced by any channel belonging to a normalized SDFG. According to this characterization, we can deduce the minimal/maximal periodic latency reachable by the normalized SDFG.

Definition 8 (Minimal/Maximal latency graph). *Let S be an optimal feasible periodic schedule for a normalized SDFG $G_{sdf} = (\mathcal{A}, E, \mathcal{P}, \mathcal{C}, M_0, \mathcal{L})$ and let $\overline{E}$ be a set of oriented arcs associated with E. For any channel $e = (a_i, a_j, p_e, c_e, M_0(e)) \in E$, let $\overline{e} = (a_i, a_j, Lat_\phi(a_i, a_j))$ be its associated arc in $\overline{E}$ where $Lat_\phi(a_i, a_j)$ is either the minimum or maximum periodic latency induced by the channel e in the schedule S. If $a_m, a_n \in \mathcal{A}$ are respectively entry and output actors of G_{sdf}, then the minimal/maximal latency graph of G_{sdf} is an oriented graph $G_\phi = (\mathcal{U}, \mathcal{V}_\phi)$ where $\mathcal{U} = \mathcal{A} \cup \{src, dst\}$, $\mathcal{V}_\phi = \overline{E} \cup \{(src, a_m, 0), (a_n, dst, 0)\}$.*

Definition 9 (Minimal/Maximal latency path). *Let consider a normalized $G_{sdf} = (\mathcal{A}, E, \mathcal{P}, \mathcal{C}, M_0, \mathcal{L})$ and let $G_\phi = (\mathcal{U}, \mathcal{V}_\phi)$ be its associated latency graph where G_ϕ (resp. $\mathcal{V}_\phi$) is either the minimal latency graph G_{min} (resp. the set of minimal latency values $\mathcal{V}_{min}$) or the maximal latency graph G_{max} (resp. the set of maximal latency values $\mathcal{V}_{max}$). Let assume that $a_m, a_n \in \mathcal{A}$ are respectively the entry and output actors of G_{sdf}. For the graph G, we define a latency path $P_i^\phi = (src, a_m, ..., a_n, dst)$ as a sequence of nodes starting from the node $src \in \mathcal{U}$ and ending to the node $dest \in \mathcal{U}$. The length of a latency path P_i^ϕ is given by:*

$$|P_i^\phi| = Lat_\phi(src, a_m) + ... + Lat_\phi(a_n, dst) \tag{8}$$

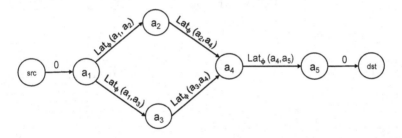

Fig. 5. The minimum/maximum latency graph G_ϕ associated with the normalized SDFG presented in Fig. 3. When $\phi = min$ (resp. $\phi = max$) then $G_\phi = G_{min}$ (resp. $G_\phi = G_{max}$) and $Lat_\phi(a_i, a_j) = Lat_{min}(a_i, a_j)$ (resp. $Lat_\phi(a_i, a_j) = Lat_{max}(a_i, a_j)$)

Figure 5 depicts the minimum/maximum latency graph associated with the normalized graph showed in Fig. 3.

The following theorem characterizes the optimal (i.e the minimal or maximal) periodic latency reachable by a normalized SDFG.

Theorem 3. *Let S be an optimal feasible periodic schedule of a normalized and connected SDFG $G_{sdf} = (\mathcal{A}, E, \mathcal{P}, \mathcal{C}, M_0, \mathcal{L})$ and let $G_{min} = (\mathcal{U}, \mathcal{V}_{min})$ and $G_{max} = (\mathcal{U}, \mathcal{V}_{max})$ be respectively its associated minimal and maximal latency graphs. For any latency path P_i^{min} of G_{min} (resp. P_i^{max} of G_{max}), the minimum (resp. maximum) periodic latency reachable by G_{sdf} is given by the minimum (resp. the maximum) latency path in G_{min} (resp. G_{max}):*

$$Lat_{min}(G_{sdf}) = \min_{i \in \mathbb{N}^*}(|P_i^{min}|). \tag{9}$$

$$Lat_{max}(G_{sdf}) = \max_{i \in \mathbb{N}^*}(|P_i^{max}|). \tag{10}$$

Proof. As weights of edges in G_{min} (resp. G_{max}) correspond to minimal latency values (resp. maximal latency values) induced by channels of G_{sdf}, the minimal latency (resp. the maximal latency) reachable by G_{sdf} is given by the shortest latency path in G_{min} (resp. the longest latency path in G_{max}). □

Minimum/maximum latency paths can be calculated in polynomial-time by traversing latency graphs from src to dst using Bellman-Ford algorithm [10]. Note that to compute the maximal latency reachable by G_{sdf} only longest latency paths are searched in G_{max}. As Bellman-Ford algorithm calculates shortest paths in directed graphs, we invert the sign of weights on edges belonging to G_{max} and then we calculate the shortest path from src to dst.

According to Theorem 3 and Fig. 4, the minimal and maximal periodic latencies reachable by the normalized graph G_{sdf} depicted in Fig. 3 are respectively given by:

$Lat_{min}(G_{sdf}) = Lat_{min}(src, a_1) + Lat_{min}(a_1, a_3) + Lat_{min}(a_3, a_4) + Lat_{min}(a_4, a_5)$
$+ Lat_{min}(a_5, dst) = 24.$
$Lat_{max}(G_{sdf}) = Lat_{max}(src, a_1) + Lat_{max}(a_1, a_2) + Lat_{max}(a_2, a_4)$
$+ Lat_{max}(a_4, a_5) + Lat_{max}(a_5, dst) = 25.$

Algorithm 1 provides the pseudo code that summarizes our latency analysis approach. The algorithm takes as input a SDFG and returns its optimal (i.e minimal or maximal) periodic latency.

Algorithm 1. Compute Optimal Periodic Latency

Input: $G_{sdf} = (\mathcal{A}, E, \mathcal{P}, \mathcal{C}, M_0, \mathcal{L})$
Output: Optimal periodic latency $Lat_\phi(G_{sdf})$
1 Normalize G_{sdf};
2 Solve the linear program (P) to determine the optimal feasible periodic
    schedule S for G_{sdf};
3 **for** $e \in E$ **do**
4 | Compute $Lat_\phi(e)$ using the schedule S and Theorem. 2 ;
5 **end**
6 Transform G_{sdf} into $G_\phi = (\mathcal{U}, \mathcal{V}_\phi)$ using Definition. 8;
7 Use Theorem. 3 and Bellman-Ford algorithm to compute $Lat^\phi(G_{sdf})$;
8 Return $Lat_\phi(G_{sdf})$;

---

5 Evaluation

In order to evaluate the effectiveness of Algorithm 1, experiments were performed by varying the size of SDFGs (i.e the number of actors) and by varying degrees (the number of edges) of actors belonging to SDFGs. To achieve this, six different tests set have been defined as a benchmark: **TS1**, **TS2**, and **TS3**, **Small**,

Medium, and **Large**. Each of these sets contains 100 connected SDFGs ran-domly generated with different parameters using Turbine[1], a multi-functional tool presented in [4] that provides fast generation of dataflow graphs.

TS1, **TS2**, and **TS3** were used to analyze the performance of the proposed algorithm when varying degrees of actors belonging to generated graphs. For any SDFG involved in these test sets, the number of actors was fixed to 300. For SDFGs contained in **TS1**, input and output degrees of actors belong to the set $\{1, 2, 3\}$. For those contained in **TS2**, they are members of $\{4, 5, 6\}$ while for those included in **TS3**, they belong to $\{7, 8, 9\}$. For any SDFGs of these sets, the execution time of actors are small (less than 10 times units) while production and consumption rates over channels are integer values between 1 and 5.

Small, **Medium**, and **Large** are test sets used for experimenting the pro-posed algorithm when varying the size of SDFGs. **Small** characterizes graphs with 100 actors, **Medium** contains graphs with 500 actors and **Huge** includes graphs with 1000 actors. For any graph of these sets, execution times of actors are also small while input and output degrees belong to the set $\{1, 2, 3\}$. Pro-duction and consumption rates over channels are also integer values between 1 and 5. The runtime of Algorithm 1 was measured for SDFGs belonging to each test set. Results were obtained on a PC Intel(R) core TM i7-7600U running at 2.80 GHz with 16 GB of RAM. Table 2 shows the minimum, maximum and ave-rage measured runtimes for the six differents test sets. Runtime for generating graphs are separated from runtimes of our latency analysis algorithm in order to have an accurate evaluation of our analysis approach. Although we can note that SDFGs belonging to the six test sets can be generated in less than 30 s with Turbine, the most interesting results are those related to Algorithm 1. Indeed, results show that runtimes of Algorithm 1 increase polynomially from **TS1** to **TS3** and from **Small** to **Huge**. This is respectively explained by the increasing variation of actors degrees and the size of SDFGs. We can particularly note that TS3 and **Huge** are clearly the most difficult test sets for our analysis approach owing to the topology of their graphs which makes Algorithm 1 time-consuming.

Table 2. Experimental results

	TS1	TS2	TS3	Small	Medium	Huge
Graph generation						
min [s]	0.68	2.49	4.53	0.09	4.35	12.38
avg [s]	3.27	6.22	13.31	0.12	5.53	12.54
max [s]	6.59	13.45	29.67	0.16	6.16	12.85
Algorithm 1						
min [s]	42.43	63.46	80.16	30.82	48.85	85.85
avg [s]	45.21	68.95	87.77	45.17	52.18	109.13
max [s]	47.46	72.33	92.14	54.82	67.93	144.06

---

[1] https://github.com/bbodin/turbine.

This time consumption is mostly related to the computation of optimal feasible periodic schedules and the search of optimal latency paths in G_ϕ which both depend on the number of edges and actors belonging to SDFGs.

From a theoretical point of view, let us consider any graph $G_{sdf} = (\mathcal{A}, E, \mathcal{P}, \mathcal{C}, M_0, \mathcal{L})$ set as input to Algorithm 1. The worst-case time complexity for normalizing G_{sdf} or transforming it into G_ϕ is constant. This complexity can be expressed as $\mathcal{O}(1)$. The computation of optimal periodic latency for channels belonging to G_{sdf} is performed in $\mathcal{O}(|E|)$ while the complexity for scheduling G_{sdf} or searching optimal latency paths that determine $Lat_\phi(G_{sdf})$ is expressed as $\mathcal{O}(|\mathcal{A}|.|E|)$. By summing these complexity measures related to the differents steps of Algorithm 1, we can express the time complexity of our latency analysis method as $\mathcal{O}(|\mathcal{A}|.|E|) + O(|E|)$. This theoretical result clearly shows that the worst-case performance of our latency analysis approach is bounded by a polynomial function.

6 Conclusion and Future Works

In this paper, we propose an analysis approach to estimating the optimal periodic latency for connected SDFGs. Experimental and theoretical results show that even if the time complexity of the approach depends on the topology of SDFGs, it is still bounded by a polynomial-time function. As future works, we plan to extend the approach in order to evaluate the optimal periodic latency reachable by the strongly connected SDFGs. We also plan to compare the performance of our approach as well as the quality of latency solutions with the approach proposed in [8] that uses self-time schedules to compute latency for SDFGs.

References

1. Zhu, X.: Work-in-progress: equivalence of transformations of synchronous data flow graphs. In: 2018 International Conference on Hardware/Software Co-design and System Synthesis (CODES+ISSS), Turin, pp. 1–2 (2018)
2. Lesparre, Y.: Efficient evaluation of mappings of dataflow applications onto distributed memory architectures. Mobile Computing, University Pierre et Marie Curie - Paris VI (2017). English
3. Khatib, J., Munier-Kordon, A., Klikpo, E.C., Trabelsi-Colibet, K.: Computing latency of a real-time system modeled by Synchronous Dataflow Graph. In: Proceedings of the 24th International Conference on Real-Time Networks and Systems (RTNS 2016), pp. 87–96. ACM, New York (2016)
4. Bodin, B., Lesparre, Y., Delosme, J.-M., Munier-Kordon, A.: Fast and efficient dataflow graph generation. In: Proceedings of the 17th International Workshop on Software and Compilers for Embedded Systems, pp. 40–49. ACM (2014)
5. Benabid-Najjar, A., Hanen, C., Marchetti, O., Munier-Kordon, A.: Periodic schedules for bounded timed weighted event graphs. IEEE Trans. Autom. Control **57**(5), 1222–1232 (2012)
6. Sriram, S., Bhattacharyya, S.S.: Embedded Multiprocessors: Scheduling and Synchronization, 2nd edn. CRC Press, Boca Raton (2009). https://doi.org/10.1201/9781420048025

7. Marchetti, O., Munier Kordon, A.: A sufficient condition for the liveness of weighted event graphs. Eur. J. Oper. Res. **197**(2), 532–540 (2009)
8. Ghamarian, A.H., Stuijk, S., Basten, T., Geilen, M.C.W., Theelen, B.D.: Latency minimization for synchronous data flow graphs. In: 10th Euromicro Conference on Digital System Design Architectures, Methods and Tools (DSD 2007), Lubeck, pp. 189–196 (2007)
9. Teruel, E., Chrzastowski-Wachtel, P., Colom, J., Silva, M.: On weighted t-systems. In: Application and Theory of Petri Nets 1992, pp. 348–367 (1992)
10. Cormen, T., Leiserson, C., Rivest, R.: Introduction to Algorithms. MIT Press, Cambridge (1990)
11. Lee, E.A., Messerschmitt, D.G.: Synchronous data flow. Proc. IEEE **75**(9), 1235–1245 (1987)

Importance-Based Scheduling to Manage Multiple Core Defection in Real-Time Systems

Yves Mouafo Tchinda[1]($\boxtimes$), Annie Choquet-Geniet[2],
and Gaëlle Largeteau-Skapin[3]

[1] CEA, LIST, Paris-Saclay, Gif-sur-yvette, France
yves.mouafo-tchinda@cea.fr
[2] LIAS, ISAE-ENSMA, Futuroscope-Chasseneuil, France
annie.geniet@univ-poitiers.fr
[3] XLIM, Université de Poitiers, Futuroscope-Chasseneuil, France
gaelle.largeteau.skapin@univ-poitiers.fr

Abstract. This paper presents an approach to support multiple permanent node failures in multicore real time systems. In the absence of failures, the system is scheduled with the PFair algorithm PD2. To overcome failures, a single spare core is provided and two protocols based on task importance are defined: The Recovery Time Distribution Protocol (RTDP) and the Graceful Degradation Protocol (GDP). When a single core fails, RTDP sets the system parameters such that all the tasks still meet their deadlines, although after a bounded delay. When several cores fail, GDP defines several modes corresponding to degraded execution. Different strategies are provided to decide which tasks are dropped in degraded modes. The experimentation of both protocols shows conclusive results. Tasks recover from the failure in a bounded delay with RTDP, whereas there are some missed deadlines with GDP. However, we exploit the experimental results to guide the designer on which elimination strategy to use.

Keywords: Real-time systems · Failure tolerance · Multicore architecture · PFair scheduling · Task importance · Mode changes

1 Introduction

The ever-growing integration of new features in real-time embedded systems requires higher computing power which leads manufacturers to migrate to more performant processors as multicore and manycore platforms. However, these platforms are exposed to physical factors which may cause the defection of one or several cores at runtime [12]. Although rare compared to temporary failures, permanent failures have more disastrous consequences because they durably reduce the processing capacities, which may result in overhead on the remaining cores and lead to missed deadlines.

© Springer Nature Switzerland AG 2019
P. Ganty and M. Kaâniche (Eds.): VECoS 2019, LNCS 11847, pp. 95–109, 2019.
https://doi.org/10.1007/978-3-030-35092-5_7

Papers dealing with fault tolerant scheduling assume that the failure detection delay is negligible, whereas this delay has an impact on the amount of lost execution to recover and thus on the scheduling results. Moreover, they apply the same recovery strategy to all tasks, whereas they do not have the same requirements: some tasks must absolutely complete before deadline, whereas some others can miss some deadlines. From the semantical point of view, some tasks must absolutely be fully processed for the sake of the security of the controlled process, whereas some others can be temporarily dropped without security issues.

The originality of this work is that the detection delay is considered and the recovery strategy is adapted to the nature of the tasks. Our problem is **how to meet task deadlines in a scheduling with single or multiple nodes defection.**

In the absence of failures, the system is scheduled with the PFair algorithm PD2 [3] which has been proven to create an optimal schedule in polynomial time. To prevent failures, two management protocols are coupled with the algorithm: the **Recovery Time Distribution Protocol (RTDP)** and the **Graceful Degradation Protocol (GDP)**. The RTDP goal is to make a single node defection transparent for the system through on-line modification of the task temporal parameters. GDP is designed to manage more than one node defection. When a failure is detected, it switches the system from its current execution mode to a degraded mode adapted to the current state of the platform. Both protocols perform using the task importance in the system. Their experimentation gives conclusive results. As expected, with RDTP, tasks which are not impacted by the failure meet their deadlines, whereas the impacted tasks recover either before deadline or before the computed recovery bound. As for GDP, some missed deadlines are recorded even for the non-impacted tasks. However, we exploit the experimental results to guide the designer on which task elimination strategy can be used for GDP optimization. Our main difficulty is to find similar works using the PFair Scheduling to compare our results.

The next section of this paper (Sect. 2) describes the considered task and failure models. It is followed by a presentation of related works (Sect. 3). Then, in Sect. 4, an overview of our approach is exposed. Sections 5 and 6 are dedicated to the presentation of RTDP and GDP respectively. In Sect. 7, we conclude and give some directions for future works.

2   Problem Specification

2.1   System Model and Scheduling Algorithm

We consider silent failure [5] and we assume a system composed of independent and periodic tasks submitted to hard temporal constraints. Each task τ_i is characterized by a worst-case execution time (WCET) C_i, a period T_i and a relative deadline D_i. A task consists of an infinite set of jobs. Deadlines are constrained when for all the tasks $D_i \leq T_i$ and implicit when $D_i = T_i$. We assume here the deadlines to be implicit. $U(\tau_i) = \frac{C_i}{T_i}$ is the task utilization and $U = \sum U(\tau_i)$ is the system load. $H = LCM(T_1...T_n)$ is the hyperperiod (where LCM is the Least Common Multiple) and $IT_k = (k - U) \times H$ is the total amount of idle time units left if the system is scheduled on k cores. In the absence of failure, the system is scheduled by the Pfair algorithm PD2 [3] which divides each task τ_i into unitary subtasks τ_i^j ($j \geq 0$). Each subtask has a pseudo-release date $r_i^j = \left\lfloor \frac{j}{U_i} \right\rfloor$ and a pseudo-deadline $d_i^j = \left\lceil \frac{j+1}{U_i} \right\rceil$ (with $j \geq 0$). The interval $[r_i^j, d_i^j)$ represents its feasibility window. Scheduling a subtask τ_i^j into its feasibility windows means that the task τ_i runs for one time unit during this time interval. A schedule of a system is *valid* if all the subtasks of its jobs are scheduled before deadline. The optimality of Pfair algorithms has been proved for systems with implicit deadlines by Baruah [4] when condition (1) is met. When the deadlines are constrained, the works in [11] give the sufficient condition (2) based on the load factor.

$$U = \sum_{i=1}^{n}(C_i/T_i) \leq k \tag{1}$$

$$CH = \sum_{i=1}^{n}(C_i/D_i) \leq k \tag{2}$$

It derives from (1) that for any given system, the minimum number of cores required for feasibility is $m = \lceil U \rceil$. According to [7] designers will size their execution platform according to this value. This paper stands in this case.

2.2   Task Importance

The validity of real-time systems is evaluated together at the functional level (i.e correctness of the results) and at the temporal level (i.e meeting the temporal constraints). Similarly, the importance of a task can be considered either from the functional or from the temporal point of view.

The **functional importance** FI_i of a task τ_i is a semantic value, which expresses the impact of its non-execution on the correctness of the results. We identify *Secondary* (S) tasks, which non-execution does not affect the results, *Preferable* (P) tasks, which non-execution leads to a degraded but acceptable results and *Vital* (V), tasks which non-execution is not acceptable since it can lead to either erroneous results or to system malfunction.

The task **temporal importance** TI_i expresses the impact of a temporal fault. It refers both to task completion and emergency. Here, a task is said *Stoppable* if the execution of some of its jobs can be suspended (i.e partially or not-executed) without leading to erroneous results. In the opposite, *Deferrable* and *Strict* tasks have to be fully completed. But some jobs of a *Deferrable* task can be completed even after the deadline (i.e a finite number of temporal faults is acceptable) while all the jobs of a *Strict* task must complete before deadline. Deferrable tasks can be assimilated to firm real-time tasks and Strict tasks to hard real-time tasks. Finally, it is important to underline that the task importance assignment is made by the designers. We assume that the temporal importance (TI_i) and the functional importance (FI_i) of each task are known.

2.3   Failure Model

We consider silent-failure [5] and we assume the existence of a health monitoring subsystem composed of a task which runs on an independent core supposed to be infallible. This core may be the one on which the operating system runs. This task records at each time unit the subtasks assigned to each core in a backup queue of size x. Then each x time unit (x being set by the designer according to the core activity), it checks the core health and updates the registers which store the state of the cores.

When a core fails, the subtasks assigned to it between t_{f_k} and t_{d_k} (where t_{f_k} and t_{d_k} respectively represent the time by which the failure occurs or is detected) are not executed, they are lost. In the worst case, there are x such lost substasks. They can belong to one or several jobs of one or several tasks. For the task τ_i, x_i denotes the number of its lost subtasks. The scheduler can access these subtasks via the backup queue and perform the reconfiguration. We assume here that $x < min(T_i)$ and thus at most one job per task has to be recovered.

3   Related Works

The standard approach to implement the failure tolerance is to use redundancy. We can mention hardware, software and temporal redundancy. Software redundancy is meant to deal with software failures, while time redundancy implies additional execution time costs. We use hardware redundancy but our goal is to limit the number of further cores. Our approach relies on two main real-time scheduling paradigms: the importance-based scheduling and the mode changes.

The Importance Based Scheduling has been introduced by Kosugi et al. [10] who proposed a method for improving the predictability of highly dynamic real time systems. In such systems, the number of tasks and their characteristics keep on changing. The authors, therefore, define the task importance as a semantic number, set by the user at design-time, and used at run-time to modify task priorities. Several other works use a synonymous concept: the value-based scheduling [2,18].

Our work, inspired by these results, proposes to use the importance, either functional or temporal, as an additional task parameter to be considered by the scheduler during failure management. The proposed types of importance differ from the one in [10], since it is not set by the user at runtime, but defined offline by the system designer. It is used only in case of failure to reorganise the system, while preserving an acceptable behavior.

Modes represent operating states of the system. A mode pools different tasks that cooperate to deliver a service. According to Burns [6], the modes of a system can be distributed into three categories. First, the **Operating modes** in which the system goes through a number of different phases regularly planned and executed. Then, the **Exceptional modes of operation** caused by rare events that lead to the execution of a code that would not have been executed if the event had not occurred. Finally, the **Degraded operating modes** caused by a failure or an error that requires the system load to be reduced and priority to be given to security and basic functionality tasks.

Mode change means that the system switches from one execution mode to another because of an internal or on external event. In our case, the trigger event will come from the health monitoring subsystem. To manage core failures, the system is reconfigured at runtime, which may involve the addition and/or removal of tasks. As in [8], a new task model (based in our case on task importance) and a new scheduling strategy are proposed to compute useful temporal parameters allowing for tasks to meet their real-time constraints. We thus define asynchronous mode change protocols [17] which allow tasks of the old and the new modes to run simultaneously during a transitional phase. Several studies have addressed the failure tolerance by mode changing, particularly for mixed-criticality systems (MCS). We can mention the works of Pathan [16] that focus on service adaptation and the scheduling of fault-tolerant MCS, and a four-mode lockstep model, developed by Al-Bayati et al. [1].

4   Overview of Our Approach

In our approach, we first want the system to be resistant to the defection of one core: the system will preserve its whole functionality and its temporal feasibility. For that aim, we define RTDP (Recovery Time Distribution Protocol), which considers task temporal importance. We use an additional spare core, which processes the tasks from the beginning of the execution. In that way, the number of time units processed before the failure is maximised, which leaves more time for the reorganisation. If several cores fail, the system will be degraded through the abandon of some tasks, in such a way that the resulting system remains feasible. Here, we use GDP (Graceful Degration Protocol), which considers task functional importance.

To manage multicores failures, we introduce 4 levels δ_X with $X \in \{SPV, PV, V, F\}$. SPV (resp. PV or V) means that all the *Secondary, Preferable* and *Vital* tasks (resp. *Preferable* and *Vital*, or only *Vital*) are considered and F means that a Failure state has been reached. We denote m_f the number of currently functional cores, and m_X the number of required cores to manage the tasks of level δ_X. For each level, we introduce several execution modes.

At each failure detection, the health monitoring subsystem informs the scheduler on the number m_f of remaining functional cores. Then, the scheduler computes the current system load U_{cur}, compares it to m_f and switches the execution to the mode corresponding to the failure level. At switch time, the non yet scheduled subtasks take their feasibility windows of the new mode.

As illustrated in Fig. 1, when the execution starts, $\delta = \delta_{SPV}$. At most one core defection is tolerable at this level and the system is in the Starting Mode. At a failure detection time, if only one core is off, RTDP is applied: the system recovers by entering the Intermediate Mode (where the lost execution is recovered) and then the Normal Mode (after recovery). When several cores have failed, the failure level becomes δ_{PV}, δ_V or δ_F. GDP is applied: the system switches either to PV-Mode or to V-Mode, which correspond to a degraded execution, or either to Failure-Mode which corresponds to system dysfunction.

The notations used in the paper are summarized in Table 1.

Table 1. Notations

t_{f_k}: occurrence time of the kth failure	t_{d_k}: detection time of the kth failure
x: failure detection delay	x_i: number of lost subtasks of τ_i
H: hyperperiod of the system	IT_k: number of idle time units on a k-cores scheduling
U: system load	m: minimal number of cores required for the system feasibility
U_X: utilisation factor induced by the tasks in X (where $X \in \{SPV, PV, V\}$)	m_X: minimal number of cores related to U_X
δ: failure level	m_f: number of remaining functional cores
β: deadline exceeding limit	I: Importance level to consider in GDP task elimination heuristics

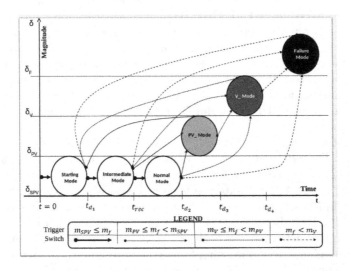

Fig. 1. Our approach: system switches to the mode adapted to the platform

5   The Recovery Time Distribution Protocol (RTDP)

Our aim is to manage the first failure in such a way that if only one core fails, the system can recover the lost execution while preserving its full functionalities. We already addressed this issue in previous works without considering task importance.

When no subtasks have been lost or the lost subtasks don't have to be recovered (according to their importance set by the designer), we proved that the addition of a single further core to the minimum required, m, provides a valid schedule. This result can be found in [13] for $x = 1$ and in [15] for $x \geq 1$. The technique is called Limited Hardware Redundancy Technique (LHRT).

In our context, it applies to systems where all the tasks are Stoppable.

When the recovery of the lost subtasks is mandatory, based on LHRT, we have proposed two techniques named the **Constrain and Release Technique** (CRT) and the **Aperiodic Flow Technique**. To perform the recovery, CRT uses a time margin preserved between task deadline and period. The constrained deadlines are computed by considering for each task a WCET of $C_i + x$ (i.e the C_i normal subtasks and x fictive substasks which is the maximum which can be lost) and $D_i = T_i$. Then, a new task deadline is obtained, considering the pseudo-deadline of the last normal subtask, i.e $D'_i = d_i^{C_i - 1}$. CRT guarantees that the deadlines are all met for systems verifying condition (2) and $T_i - C_i \geq x$.

AFT exploits idle time units to recover the lost substasks. These time units are identified at runtime as the substasks of an additional idle task τ_{id} ($C_{id} = IT_m$ and $T_{id} = H$) which is scheduled together with the other tasks. AFT tolerates a few deadlines to be missed, but guarantees that the system will have recovered not later than β time units after the failure detection (with $\beta = \left\lceil \frac{x+2}{U_{\tau_{id}}} \right\rceil$).

In our context, CRT applies when all the tasks are *Strict* and AFT when they are all *Deferrable*. Both techniques are presented in [14] for $x = 1$ and [15] for $x \geq 1$.

One of the weaknesses of LHRT, CRT and AFT is that their application is limited to system composed of tasks of the same temporal importance. Thus, the same recovery strategy is applied to all the tasks. Here, we mixed the three techniques to get a flexible technique which can be applied to a larger range of feasible systems, composed together of *Stoppable*, *Deferrable* and *Strict* tasks. The goal of RTDP is to distribute the recovery time to the impacted tasks according to their requirements, which depend on the importance.

Let $S : \tau_i <C_i, T_i, TI_i, FI_i>$ be the system to schedule. When the first core defection is detected, for each impacted task τ_i:

- if $TI_i = Sp$ (i.e τ_i is *Stoppable*), since a partial completion of its jobs is tolerable, its lost subtasks are not rescheduled;
- if $TI_i = St$ (i.e τ_i is *Strict*), since a full completion of its jobs before the deadline is mandatory, its lost subtasks are rescheduled in the preserved margin;
- if $TI_i = Df$ (i.e τ_i is *Defferable*), since a full completion of its jobs even later is mandatory, its lost subtasks are rescheduled in the idle time units using an aperiodic flow.

5.1   The Execution Modes

RTDP defines three execution modes composed each of all the tasks to be scheduled but with different parameters. We adopt the pattern $<C_i, D_i, T_i>$ to describe task WCET, deadline and period in each mode. We have the following modes (see Fig. 1):

- **The Starting Mode:** *Stoppable* tasks: $<C_i, T_i, T_i>$;
  Strict tasks: $<C_i, D'_i, T_i>$ $(D'_i < T_i$ is computed as in CRT to preserve a time margin); *Defferable* tasks: $<C_i, T_i, T_i>$.
  We assume that the System S_S composed of the tasks of the Starting Mode meets the feasibility condition (2) on $m + 1$ cores.
- **The Intermediate Mode:** *Stoppable* tasks: $<C_i, T_i, T_i>$ for the non impacted tasks and $<C_i - x_i, T_i, T_i>$ for the impacted tasks; *Strict* tasks: $<C_i, T_i, T_i>$ for the non impacted tasks and $<C_i + x_i, T_i, T_i>$ for the impacted tasks; *Defferable* tasks:$<C_i, T_i, T_i>$; Idle task τ_{id}: $<IT_m, H, H>$; Aperiodic flow Fl: $< \sum x_i, \infty, \infty>$ (all the *Defferable* lost substasks).
  We assume that the System S_I composed of the tasks of the Intermediate Mode meets the feasibility condition (1) on m cores.
- **The Normal Mode:** *Stoppable, Strict* and *Defferrable*: $<C_i, D_i, T_i>$ (initial parameters); Idle task τ_{id}: $<IT_m, H, H>$ (kept for further recovery of both *Strict* and *Defferable* lost subtasks). Aperiodic flow task Fl: $<0, \infty, \infty>$ (empty but will be used if a new failure occurs).
  We assume that the initial System S composed of the tasks of the Normal Mode meets the feasibility condition (1) on m cores.

The execution begins in the Starting Mode and substask feasibility windows are computed with PD2 considering the system S_S. If no failure occurs, the execution ends in this mode. But, if a failure occurs and a single node is off, the system switches to the Intermediate Mode and the non yet scheduled substasks take their feasibility windows computed with the system S_I. The next hyperperiod, after recovery, the system naturally enters the Normal Mode with feasibility windows computed with the initial system S.

5.2   Example

Let's consider the following system S $(\tau_i < C_i, D_i, T_i, TI_i, FI_i >)$:

$\tau_1 < 1, 3, 3, S_p, S>$, $\tau_2 < 2, 6, 6, D_f, P>$, $\tau_3 < 2, 4, 4, S_t, V>$,
$\tau_4 < 5, 12, 12, D_f, S>$, $\tau_5 < 3, 12, 12, S_t, P>$, $\tau_6 < 4, 12, 12, S_p, P>$,
$\tau_7 < 2, 6, 6, S_t, V>$, $\tau_8 < 7, 12, 12, S_p, S>$, $\tau_9 < 1, 4, 4, D_f, S>$,
$\tau_{10} < 1, 6, 6, S_t, P>$.
$H = 12$. $U_{SPV} = \frac{42}{12} = 3.5 \Rightarrow m_{SPV} = 4$; $U_{PV} = 1.91$, $m_{PV} = 2$; $U_V = 0.83$,
$m_V = 1$. $IT_4 = (4 - \frac{42}{12}) \times 12 = 6$.

At the beginning of the execution, $m_f = m + 1 = 5 > m_{SPV}$ and thus $\delta = \delta_{SPV}$. We consider $x = 2$. To preserve a time margin for *Strict* tasks recovery, constrained deadlines are considered and the execution starts with the following parameters for *Strict* tasks $\tau_3 < 2, 2, 4, S_t, V>$, $\tau_5 < 3, 8, 12, S_t, P>$, $\tau_7 < 2, 4, 6, S_t, V>$, $\tau_{10} < 1, 2, 6, S_t, P>$. The other tasks keep their initial parameters. The load factor is $CH(S_S) = \frac{103}{24} = 4.29 < m_f$ and thus condition (2) is met.

We now consider a first failure occurring at time $t_p = 5$ on one core. We have $m_f = 4 = m_{SPV}$ and thus $\delta = \delta_{SPV}$. The idle task $\tau_{id}<6, 12, 12, S_t, P>$ is added to the system to identify and fairly distribute idle time units. Since the failure is detected after $x = 2$ time units, the subtasks τ_5^1 and τ_9^5 assigned to the failing core are not scheduled. Since τ_5^1 belongs to the first job of the *Strict* task τ_5, it will be rescheduled within the preserved time margin $[8, 12)$. As for the *Deferrable* subtask τ_9^5, it is added to an aperiodic flow and will be rescheduled at the place of the idle subtask τ_{id}^3. The shedule is valid since the lost subtasks are recovered before deadline.

5.3 Experimental Results

To evaluate the approach, we have designed a software prototype composed of three modules. The first module is a system generator, which randomly generates systems in compliance with the approach conditions. The number of tasks per system ranges from 5 to 20 and the periods are chosen so that the hyperperiod is limited to 210 using the Goossens method [9]. Then, the task's WCET is uniformly chosen between 1 and the period. Both temporal and functional importances are randomly set. At each iteration, 550 systems are generated grouped into 11 categories. Each category corresponds to a percentage of heavy tasks (a task τ is heavy if $u(\tau_i) > 0.5$) in the system. This categorization is motivated by the fact that the recovery time, particularly for *Strict* tasks, depends on the processor utilization. The higher the utilization, the later the lost subtasks are recovered. In our experiments, the percentage of heavy tasks varies from 0 to 100 with a step of 10. The second module is a simulator which applies the approach to each generated system and stores the obtained schedule. The failure times and the failing cores are randomly chosen. The detection delay varies from 1 to 5. Finally, the last module analyses the schedules and provides some performance results. We study the first two hyper-periods: we assume failures to occur during the first hyper-period and we observe the system recovery until the second hyperperiod.

RTDP have been experimented with our prototype. The protocol is applied 10 times on the same group of systems to vary the failure time and the failing core (and thus the impacted tasks). The analysis module has evaluated the schedule validity and, in the cases of missed deadlines, the respect of the limit β. The global results reveal that in 40% of the cases, systems scheduled with RTDP are valid, i.e all the impacted tasks, including the *Deferrable*, recover their lost subtasks before the deadlines. Furthermore, missed deadlines only concern the impacted instances of *Deferrable* tasks and these instances recover before the limit. These results correspond to the expectations and thus validate the protocol.

5.4 Sketch of Proof

We already proved that dropping some (sub)tasks doesn't cause any temporal faults ([13]), so stoppable tasks don't miss their deadlines. Next, we proved that due to the time margin, the strict tasks meet their deadlines too ([14]). As to the deferrable tasks, we can consider that the concerned subtasks are dropped, which again doesn't cause any deadline passing. Then we showed ([15]) that the tasks within the aperiodic flow always recover after a bounded delay β. The experiments only highlighted those points.

6   The Graceful Degradation Protocol (GDP)

The principle of GDP is to switch the system from its current execution mode to a degraded mode corresponding to the platform modification in order to keep the condition (1) satisfied. The problem is then to discriminate between the tasks to know which ones will be executed or not in the new mode. For that, GDP exploits task functional importance to manage task elimination while keeping the most functionalities.

6.1   The GDP Execution Modes

The GDP defines four execution modes:

- The **PV-Mode**, which corresponds to δ_{PV}. The system switches to this mode if, at a failure detection time, $m_{PV} \leq m_f < m_{SPV}$, i.e the number of functional cores does not longer ensure the system feasibility, but it can ensure the feasibility of the *Preferable* and the *Vital* tasks. It is a degraded version of any of the RTDP modes obtained by eliminating some *Secondary* tasks.
- The **V-Mode**, which corresponds to the δ_V. The system switches to this mode if, at a failure detection time, $m_V \leq m_f < m_{PV}$, i.e the number of functional cores does not longer ensure the system feasibility, but can only ensure the feasibility of the *Vital* tasks. It is a degraded version of the PV-Mode. It can be obtained from PV-Mode by eliminating some *Preferable* tasks or from the δ_{SPV} mode by eliminating all the *Secondary* and some *Preferable* tasks.
- The **Failure-Mode** is the most degradated mode corresponding to δ_F. The system switches to this mode if $m_f < m_V$, i.e at a failure detection time, the number of functional cores cannot even ensures the feasibility of the *Vital* tasks. It can be obtained from any of other modes by eliminating all the *Secondary* and *Preferable* tasks, as well as the idle task. Moreover, in this mode, the lost subtasks are no longer recovered.

6.2   Mode Changing

At any failure detection time:

- if $m_f \geq m_{SPV}$ then $\delta = \delta_{SPV}$: the system is kept in its current execution mode; no task is eliminated and RTDP takes over;
- if $m_{PV} \leq m_f < m_{SPV}$ then $\delta = \delta_{PV}$: the system is switched to PV-Mode by eliminating some *Secondary* tasks until $U_{cur} \leq m_f$; the lost subtasks of the non eliminated tasks are added to the aperiodic flow;
- if $m_V \leq m_f < m_{PV}$ then $\delta = \delta_V$: the system is switched to V-Mode first by eliminating all the *Secondary* tasks and then some *Preferable* tasks until $U_{cur} \leq m_f$; the lost subtasks of the non eliminated tasks are added to the aperiodic flow;

– if $m_f < m_V$ then $\delta = \delta_F$: the system is switched to Failure Mode. The system can no longer deliver a minimum service and therefore it is defective. The idle task is deleted, all the lost subtasks are abandoned and the flow is emptied.

In the PV-Mode and the V-Mode, U_{cur} and m_f are computed without taking into account the idle task τ_{id}. Then, their new values are used to calculate the amount of idle time units and to set the τ_{id} WCET. Afterward, τ_{id} is added to the system for the recovery: the subtasks of the aperiodic flow are processed each time an subtask of τ_{id} is scheduled.

6.3   Task Elimination Heuristics

Two objectives can be targeted when eliminating tasks: maximizing the residual load and/or minimizing the number of dropped tasks. These problems turn out to be bin packing problems which are known to be NP-complete. Hence we rely on heuristics. For the first objective, two heuristics are proposed: the Lightest Task Heuristic (H1) and the Marginal Task Heuristic (H2). For the second objective, the Number of Remaining Tasks Heuristic (H3) is proposed.

The principle of H1 is, at each iteration, to eliminate the task with the lowest utilization among those whose functional importance is I (where I is the functional importance of the tasks to drop) until the condition (1) is met again on m_f. This is performed by Algorithm 1. For example, if we consider the system S of Sect. 5.2 and if a second failure affecting three other cores is detected, $m_f = 1$ but $U_{cur} = 3.5$. At the first iteration, $I = S$ and H1 will eliminate τ_1, τ_4 and τ_9. At the second iteration, $I = P$ and τ_2, τ_5, τ_6 and τ_{10} are eliminated. We then have $U_{cur} = 1.58 < m_f$.

H2 first computes the gap between the system load and the number of functional cores. At each iteration, a set of tasks whose functional importance equals I is formed. Then, the heaviest task of this set within those having an utilization less than or equal to the gap is eliminated and the gap is updated. This is performed by the Algorithm 2. For a second failure which affects two other cores during the execution of the system S of Sect. 5.2, H2 eliminates τ_8 and τ_9 at its first iteration and τ_1, τ_5 and τ_{10} at the second iteration. We then have $U_{cur} = 1.91 < m_f$.

The idea of H3 is to eliminate the lightest task among those which utilization is greater than or equal to the gap. If no such task exists, the heaviest task which functional importance equals I is eliminated. This can be expressed by

---

Algorithm 1. Lightest Task Heuristic

repeat
  eliminate τ_l, the lightest task with $FI_l = I$;
  $U_{cur} \leftarrow U_{cur} - U(\tau_l)$;
  $gap \leftarrow U_{cur} - m_f$;
until $(gap \leq 0) \vee (\{\tau_i / FI_i = I\} = \emptyset)$;

Algorithm 3. For a second failure which affects two other cores during the execution of the system S of Sect. 5.2, H3 eliminates τ_4 and τ_8 at its first iteration and τ_1 and τ_5 at the second iteration. We then have $U_{cur} = 1.91 < m_f$.

Algorithm 2. Marginal Task Heuristic

$gap \leftarrow U_{cur} - m_f$;
repeat
 | $\tau_{vict} \leftarrow \tau_v$ such that $U(\tau_v) = max(U(\tau))$ with $FI_v = I \wedge U(\tau) \leq gap)$;
 | eliminate(τ_{vict});
 | $U_{cur} \leftarrow U_{cur} - U(\tau_{vict})$;
 | $gap \leftarrow U_{cur} - m_f$;
until $(gap \leq 0) \vee (\{\tau_i, U(\tau_i) \leq gap \wedge FI_i = I\} = \emptyset)$;
if $(gap > 0) \wedge (\{\tau_i / FI_i = I\} \neq \emptyset)$ **then**
 | $\tau_{vict} \leftarrow$ the remaining ligthest task;
 | eliminate(τ_{vict});
 | $U_{cur} \leftarrow U_{cur} - U(\tau_{vict})$;

else
 | no solution

Algorithm 3. Number of Remaining Tasks Heuristic

$gap \leftarrow U_{cur} - m_f$;
repeat
 | $V \leftarrow \{\tau_i / FI_i = I \wedge (U(\tau_i) \geq gap)\}$;
 | **if** $V \neq \emptyset$ **then**
 | | eliminate the ligthest task in V;

 | **else**
 | | eliminate the heaviest task which importance equals I;

 | $gap \leftarrow U_{cur} - m_f$;
until $(gap < 0) \vee (\{\tau_i / FI_i = I\} = \emptyset)$;

6.4   Experimental Results

GDP has been experimented following the scenario described in Sect. 5.3. Each system in a group has been scheduled using each of the heuristic and the three obtained schedules are compared to each other according to three criteria: the number of missed deadlines metric (MDM), the residual load metric (RLM) and the number of remaining tasks metric (RTM). An heuristic is the best for MDM if it provides the lowest number of missed deadlines in the schedule. It is the best for RLM if it provides the greatest value of system load after task elimination. Finally, an heuristic is best for RTM if it keeps the maximal number of non eliminated tasks. During each test, we have computed for each group the number of systems for which each heuristic is the best for a given metric. The cases when several heuristics have the same performances are included in the results. This explains why the sum of the three values can be greater than the number of systems (50 here). Figure 2 shows the results for MDM. It follows that there is no system among the 550 tested for which H3 has the lowest number of the missed deadlines. The best performance for this metric is obtained with H1 for systems composed of less than 80% of heavy tasks and with H2 for systems having more than 90%.

The results for RLM are presented in Fig. 3. We can observe that for all the groups, H3 has the best performances. Otherwise, H1 is more performant than H2 for system which heavy tasks rate is between 50% and 80%.

As for RTM, the results of Fig. 4 confirm that H3 is the heuristic which always keeps the maximum number of non eliminated tasks, hence its name. Moreover, H2 has better performances than H1 for this metric.

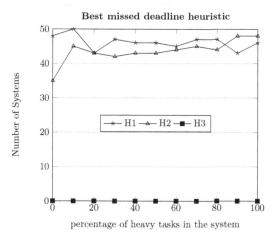

Fig. 2. Heuristic performance evolution for the missed deadline metric

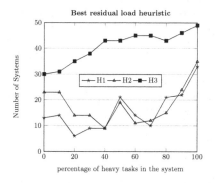

Fig. 3. Heuristic performance evolution for the residual load metric

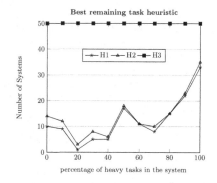

Fig. 4. Heuristic performance evolution for the remaining tasks metric

7   Conclusion and Perspectives

To adapt a multicore real-time system to the modification of its execution environment, we have proposed two protocols based on task importance, which can be coupled with a PFair scheduling to manage one or multiple core defection. For a single core defection, the Recovery Time Distribution Protocol (RTDP) gives excellent experimental results in that the tasks which are not affected by the failure meet their deadlines and the affected tasks recover in a bounded delay.

The Graceful Degradation Protocol (GDP) is designed to handle multiple core defections with three degraded execution modes. A new mode is built by eliminating some tasks of the former mode until the system is feasible again. We have proposed three heuristics to perform task elimination, while preserving a highest residual load and as much as possible the system functionalities.

In future works, we intend to further validate RTDP and GDP. For RTDP, we want to study gap between the recovery bound and the response time to see whether this bound is overestimated and thus must be adjusted. As for GDP, we will analyse the gap between two heuristic performances for each metric. This may help the designers to choose an heuristic with relevant performances for the three metrics. Finally, from the second core defection, GDP manages the recovery of the *Strict* tasks in the same way as that of the *Deferrable* tasks. We intend to propose a management policy adapted to *Strict* tasks.

References

1. Al-bayati, Z., Caplan, J., Meyer, B.H., Zeng, H.: A four-mode model for efficient fault-tolerant mixed-criticality systems. In: Proceedings of the 2016 Conference on Design, Automation and Test in Europe, pp. 97–102 (2016)
2. Aldarmi, S.A., Burns, A.: Dynamic value-density for scheduling real-time systems. In: Proceedings of the 11th Euromicro Conference on R.T. S., pp. 270–277 (1999)
3. Anderson, J.H.: A new look at PFair priorities. Technical report, Department of Computer Science, University of North Carolina (1999)
4. Baruah, S.K., Cohen, N.K., Plaxton, C.G., Varvel, D.A.: Proportionate progress: a notion of fairness in resource allocation. Algorithmica $15(6)$, 600–625 (1996)
5. Brasileiro, F.V., Ezhilchelvan, P.D., Shrivastava, S.K., Speirs, N.A., Tao, S.: Implementing fail-silent nodes for distributed systems. IEEE Trans. Comput. $45(11)$, 1226–1238 (1996)
6. Burns, A.: System mode changes-general and criticality-based (2014)
7. Choquet-Geniet, A., Largeteau-Skapin, G.: Size analysis in multiprocessor real-time scheduling. Int. J. Crit. Comput. Based Syst. **6**, 197–217 (2014)
8. Gammoudi, A., Benzina, A., Khalgui, M., Chillet, D.: Energy-efficient scheduling of real-time tasks in reconfigurable homogeneous multi-core platforms. IEEE Trans. Syst. Man, Cybern. Syst. 1–14 (2018). https://doi.org/10.1109/TSMC.2018.2865965. https://hal.inria.fr/hal-01934955
9. Goossens, J., Macq, C.: Limitation of the hyper-period in real-time periodic task set generation. In: Proceedings of the RTS Embedded System, pp. 133–147 (2001)
10. Kosugi, N., Mitsuzawa, A., Tokoro, M.: Importance-based scheduling for predictable real-time systems using MART. In: Proceedings of the 4th International Workshop on Parallel and Distributed Real-Time Systems, WPDRTS, pp. 95–100 (1996)

11. Malo, S., Choquet-Geniet, A., Bikienga, M.: PFair scheduling of late released tasks with constrained deadlines. In: 4e Colloque National sur la Recherche en Informatique et ses Applications, pp. 142–149 (2012)
12. Mottaghi, M.H., Zarandi, H.R.: DFTS: a dynamic fault-tolerant scheduling for real-time tasks in multicore processors. Microprocess. Microsyst. **38**(1), 88–97 (2014)
13. Mouafo Tchinda, Y., Choquet-Geniet, A., Largeteau-Skapin, G.: Failure tolerance for a multicore real-time system scheduled by PD2. In: Proceedings of the 9th Junior Researcher Workshop on Real-Time Computing, JRWRTC 2015, pp. 1–4 (2015)
14. Mouafo Tchinda, Y., Geniet-Choquet, A., Largeteau-Skapin, G.: Dynamic feasibility windows reconfiguration for a failure-tolerant PFair scheduling. In: Proceedings of the 10th Workshop on Verification and Evaluation of Computer and Communication System, VECoS 2016, Tunis, Tunisia, 6–7 October 2016, pp. 61–76 (2016)
15. Mouafo Tchinda, Y., Largeteau-Skapin, G., Choquet Geniet, A.: Multicore scheduling of real-time systems subject to permanent failure of one core with detection delay. Int. J. Crit. Comput. Based Syst. **8**, 258 (2018)
16. Pathan, R.M.: Fault-tolerant and real-time scheduling for mixed-criticality systems. Real Time Syst. **50**(4), 509–547 (2014)
17. Real, J., Crespo, A.: Mode change protocols for real-time systems: a survey and a new proposal. Real Time Syst. **26**(2), 161–197 (2004)
18. Swaminathan, S.: Value-based scheduling in real-time systems. Ph.D. thesis, Iowa State University (2002)

Author Index

Printed in the United States
By Bookmasters